THE FULFILLED RETIREE

A Complete Guide to Build a Retirement Full of Purpose, Achieve Financial Independence, Health, and Meaningful Hobbies for a Joyful Retirement Life You'll Truly Enjoy

Jude Nathaniel

Copyright

Copyright © 2024 *Jude Nathaniel.*

All rights reserved. No part of this book may be reproduced in any form by an electronic or mechanical means, including information storage and retrieval systems, without permission in writing from the publisher, except by a reviewer who may quote brief passages in a review.

Contents

THE FULFILLED RETIREE 1
Copyright..2
Contents..3
Introduction 6
Description 16
Chapter 1...18
   Imagining A Perfect Retirement..18
      How to Create Financial Goals 22
CHAPTER 2 28
   How to Calculate your Retirement Number 28
CHAPTER 3 38
   Budgeting for the Long Haul 38
Chapter 4...50
   Investment Strategies for Security 50
      Six Low-Risk Investments for Retirees 52
CHAPTER 5 60
   Monthly Income Planning Strategy 60
      How to Find Your Income Needs 61
      Balancing Passive and Active Income 65
      How to Properly Manager your Income 68
CHAPTER 6 72
   Healthcare and Insurance Planning 72
      How to Budget and Plan Your Expenses. 78
CHAPTER 7 84

Tax-Sensitive Withdrawals Strategies 84
    Taxable, Tax-Deferred and Tax-Free Accounts 85
    How to Optimize Tax Reduction on the Withdrawal Process 88

CHAPTER 8 96
    Making the Right Retirement Housing Decisions 96
    How Relocating Affects Your Finances 100

CHAPTER 9 106
    How to Protect Your Assets in Retirement 106

CHAPTER 10 116
    How to Live Healthy in Retirement 116
    (Physically, Emotionally and Mentally) 116
        How to Live A Healthy, Physically Active Life 117
        Caring for the Mind and Emotions 120

CHAPTER 11 128
    Achieving Financial Freedom in Retirement 128
        Understanding Financial Freedom During Retirement 129
        How to Stay Financially Independent and not depend on your Family 133

CHAPTER 12 138
    How to Gain Cheap Travel Budget in Retirement 138
        How To Create a Realistic Travel Budget 139
        Travel Planning Without Breaking the Bank 144

CHAPTER 13 148
    Adapting to Inflation in Retirement 148
        1. Risk Reduction through Diversified Investments 151

Strategies for Financial Resilience Over a Lifetime 155

CHAPTER 13 158

Adapting Technology in Retirement 158

CHAPTER 14 168

Living a Grateful and Content Life in Retirement 168

CHAPTER 15 178

Best Investment Options to Consider When Approaching Retirement Age 178

CHAPTER 16 186

How to Spot & Avoid Wrong Investments 186

Best Ways to Safeguard Your Investments 192

Introduction

Welcome! Retirement is a path we all must travel, and for some, the anticipation builds excitement, while others are intrigued by where it may take them. We all fantasize about life when we finally break free from the work treadmill that has held us in place for years. As we open up this introduction, let us also dive into what you are hoping to accomplish and how you see the journey of your retirement shaping up. In partnership, we will map the possible outcomes of your retirement world and realize those dreams with specific actions that will lead you on track for a satisfying and fulfilling post-work life. One key point that I think is worth repeating is that retirement isn't just leaving work; it's hitting a reset so you can plan what matters most in your days. This book can help you plan a purposeful and financially secure journey, whether your retirement dreams are about hopping on an RV to visit all of the National Parks or enjoying time with family after decades in the workforce. This journey is about rediscovering yourself and a golden era of Getting to live life your way. Retirement is not only about money; though you might think that from so many other sources Available in Prioritize & Invest for Retirement, this book will delve into the personal and psychological aspects of retirement planning. There is also a section on creating SMART goals and drawing up your roadmap to guide you daily with clarity, confidence, and peace of mind.

How to Use This Book

Consider each chapter like a piece of construction work. We will help you from the beginning, guiding you to visualize your ideal retirement through budgeting and investment strategies down to home health tips for living fully while staying safe. Every chapter gets you one step further into creating a retirement plan that seems doable and fun. By the end, you will walk away with a complete set of strategies, lessons, and tangible advice that meets your needs.

Here are the Three Long-Term Care Protocols of Retirement Success in Action

First, we have to define a "successful" retirement. Based on my experience, I argue that the three central objectives to focus on are financial security, emotional gratification, and purpose. When these three pillars are balanced, retirement will become less of a winding down and more likened to a renaissance for the individual.

1. *Financial Security*

What makes someone feel financially secure varies from person to person. For others, it is sufficient to have a stable income that pays the bills and leaves some room for dining or unforeseen expenses. For some, it is legacy – preserving a loved one or philanthropic giving. A solid financial foundation is the cornerstone of this because it will enable you to make decisions based on what YOU want, not some outlook. Each lesson you will go through will help you identify what YOU want and learn how to create a financial plan that fits your personal goals.

2. *Emotional Fulfillment*

Retirement is a great time to reacquaint yourself, find out what interest you may have put on the back burner through life, and build relationships with friends and family. However, emotional fulfillment comes into play not just through activities but also by taking pleasure in all our daily activities. We will get into self-care and personal support, e.g., if you... This includes volunteering following a hobby or meeting friends as a new tribe)

3. *A Sense of Purpose*

Even more important, it is essential to have a cause, no matter how old we are. With the structure and work-like nature of our previous days, it might feel challenging at first to come into more open daytimes. It will suggest strategies for building purpose, even through lifelong learning of new skills, serving as a caregiver to an elderly parent, or starting on long-delayed personal projects. Once you know what motivates you and makes you feel most fulfilled, retirement can be a fulfilling part of life — not just an extended holiday.

What Can Goals Do for Retirement?

The book advises setting particular goals, so let us define what that means in retirement planning. Goals serve as the guiding star on a twisting road of retirement.

Career goals often fit into fixed timelines with markers you either reach, beat, or fall short of—retirement goals are broader and more individual, reflecting where your values lie, what dreams make sleep even sweeter for you, and how style matters.

Take A Look at Some Retirement Goals You Might Consider:

1. Financial Goals:

- Making X amount a month/year

– Economically to save where necessary without affecting quality of life

- Establishing a fund for emergencies.

2. Lifestyle Goals:

- Moving or Downsizing

- Traveling to places that you have always wanted to.

- More time on hobbies — painting, gardening, or read

3. Health and Wellness Goals:

- Keeping active physically by doing structured workouts

- Eating a nutritious diet that meets your unique nutrition requirements

- Meditation, mindfulness, or other mental health exercises to stay strong and agile

4. Legacy Goals:

- Leaving your inheritance for the next generation

- Being Charitable or Building a Legacy (like Ancestry.com Family Tree)

- Telling your life story, leaving a legacy of stories – including sharing family values

- Writing through generations and remembering loved ones

Each chapter has guidance and actionable steps to make these goals achievable. Establishing your goals and checking in regularly can help ensure you will never lose sight of living a happy retirement.

What to Expect in Every Chapter:

Every Chapter in this book is organized in a simple format: it starts with an overview of the topic and practical recommendations, and some chapters may have checklists or workouts. And I try to use real-life stories when available so that we can relate the lessons back and through personal experiences. A brief description of what each section contains is as follows:

1. *Lesson Overview:* A short explanation of this lesson and why it is important

2. *Main Idea:* Every chapter will cover the key points. These short, oh-and-ah generalizations are valuable if you need to get directly into high gear.

3. *Action Steps:* A few chapters offer exercises to show you how to put the lesson into practice in your own life. These are low-hanging fruit to account for and are easily and doable retirement planning.

4. *My Opinion:* I encourage you to reflect on retirement occasionally. This will help you keep track of what changes and tweaks will be necessary on your journey.

Personalizing Your Retirement Journey

Please read the book, take notes as you go along, and personalize it to apply. Everyone's path to retirement is different, so feel free to use a model that fits all. While it certainly provides a guide, ultimately, you are in control.

The chapters are filled with simple but nugget-sized hints that are easy to digest and use.

Reflect After Every Session: Consider what you have learned and how it can be applied after the lecture. What resonates with you? What goals stand out? This time of reflection will provide you with some severe clarity and focus.

Pick Your Battles: You can skip each recommendation in a book. Take what resonates with you and ignore the rest. Retirement is a personal journey, and bypassing some components that might not align with your objectives is okay.

Chat with Loved Ones: Discuss your retirement planning in a friendly manner on weekend brunch or at the family gathering. Sharing your wisdom helps keep you focused on where you're heading but can also invite some support and inspiration.

We will start with the first step in the next chapter, which is seeing your retirement lifestyle. This is a rich exercise for converting abstract ideas into plans; it will help you understand what you need. As I work with clients on retirement planning, we often discover a few rules of thumb and more about values: what you enjoy in your life, how fulfillment looks for you, talked through peace of mind.

Chatting with you has given us a surge of inspiration...and some things to discuss on tips for creating a retirement lifestyle that fits the way YOU want to live. With all this in mind, take out your pen and paper or laptops/computers/tablets (in other words, get ready!).

Description

Are you prepared to experience your best financial (emotional and mental) retirement years? From early planning to retirement, this book has everything you need to manage your way through each step of modern aging. Picture your retired life as part of the plot loaded with opportunities to fill it by discovering, loosening up, and extensively appreciating, having no monetary issues or questions concerning what is on the horizon. Written conversationally, *The Fulfilled Retiree* offers clearcut answers to the most pressing questions facing every pre- and post-retiree: As it stands now… will I outlive my investments? So, what investments should I be doing now? How do I stay fit, healthy, and social? Even more critical — how do I structure my life to find a mission and fulfillment? Based on the 2024 financial forecasts, every chapter provides what you need to do right now to back up or improve your investment and retirement spending framework.

This book will prepare you to make informed, effective decisions that can support your lifestyle and goals well into the future — from recognizing the best investment strategies for years where returns are unlikely to be attractive or easy to know how much in equities is "enough" (and what could happen if you believe there's never too much); spotting one good, bad investment...and when buying a $2 lottery ticket might not be worse than funding an HSA.

The Fulfilled Retiree is more than just about the financial aspects. Ultimately, this book acknowledges that the profound side of a happy and fulfilling retirement lies in building emotional well-being, health & happiness. You will get hands-on skills to keep the body moving, connect social circles, and deep dive into gratitude as a daily practice for human fulfillment.

Keep turning the page to a new chapter of readiness and excitement for whatever is next. Retirement can be one of the most rewarding times in your life — let Retirement Redefined help show you how!

Chapter 1

Imagining A Perfect Retirement

Close your eyes and visualize where you will be in five, ten, or twenty years. You are getting up without an alarm clock. The day is ahead, and your decisions will decide how it unfolds. What do you see? Is it a peaceful morning on your sun porch with some coffee and an excellent book, or is it an eventful day volunteering in your community, sightseeing around the globe, or being with family? Only then can you be sure your destination is worth the work to arrive there and that arrival will set up a retirement of fulfillment and purpose? Many people float into retirement without a clear. The idea of what they want and find themselves emotionally stagnating, feeling like, "Is that it?" This cannot be you. This chapter is devoted to assisting you with envisioning something that generates inspiration for your vision design that feels authentic and consistent with who you are based on current personality psychology. Your vision may be a bit fuzzy initially, which is OK. Retirement brings an excellent life transformation, and it is so difficult to know what we want in our lives without work comprising the rest of them.

Step 1: Create an image of what your retirement day would look like

Create an image of what the "perfect" day in retirement would be. Be as specific as you can with your content. What about waking up in the morning — what kind of day awaits?

Questions that Will Guide you through Painting this Picture:

Q- *What is the first thing you do when you wake up?*

Are you at home, on vacation, or even in a new, different part of the world?

– Do you have people around you ... husband, family, friends or neighbors?

– How do you spend your day? Do you have any hobbies, creative activities, part-time jobs, volunteering, or learning something new?

Q — What are your evenings like? How do you imagine spending time with friends, family, or nothing else but in solitude?

Don't worry about whether your vision is realistic or attainable when answering these questions. This is the stage of dreaming — for your mind to roam and wander — however fanciful it may be. Week 10— Free yourself from believing your dream isn't practical. The more radical and world-changing, the more likely it is to happen. comments

Step 2: Define Your Individual Goals

When you have a general idea of your ideal "perfect day," expand on this vision and create concrete personal goals. Goals chart your path through retirement years and direct you toward experiences that fit you well.

Some Personal goals to consider:

- Lifestyle goals:

Do you want to move, downsize, or even live part of the year in another country? Do you have a home renovation or purchase in mind that can improve your daily life and the lives of others?

- Health Goals:

Do you want to follow a fitness or wellness routine? What about yoga, meditation, or checking off that marathon from your bucket list?

- Learning and Growth:

Are there interests in which you wish to expand or develop skills? It could be cooking or painting. Perhaps you are going to decide to get a new degree.

- Community Involvement:

Volunteering and helping others can be advantageous. Do you have a favorite charity that needs your help?

- Relationships:

Many people dream about having more time with their family and loved ones at home when they retire. Is there anyone you should spend more time with — old friends, your grandchildren?

Write these down in a journal. As always, all goals are good ones, not great ones or wrong goals... only what is true to you. Throughout this process, you will learn a lot about what will bring happiness to the new part of your life.

Step 3: Building Financial Goals to Facilitate Your Vision

You are so moving to finances and houses. We all have retirement dreams, but they don't come cheap. If you dream of traveling a lot, you will need travel money; if moving out — as in renting or buying a new place to live) wokidly transplant your things without needing movers?). Creating financial targets that align with your life plan will enable you to retire energized and respectful.

How to Create Financial Goals

- Know your estimated monthly expenditures

Begin with a ballpark figure. What is the amount you require to live a comfortable life every month? Consider basic housing, utilities, food and medical needs, and discretionary spending like entertainment. Also, plan for inflation; things that cost X today will cost more.

- Account for One-Time Expenses

Plan for One-Time Big Expenses — While you cannot plan for every expense that comes your way, some one-time expenses, such as home renovations, a big vacation, or a new car in the next year, should be laid out within your financial blueprint. List these costs and think about when you are going to have those. Continual monitoring helps prevent unexpected events that would derail your retirement income.

- Set Income Goals

Check on your potential income streams like Social Security, pension (if any), retirement savings, or investments. Establish an income goal that ties in with your expenditures and delivers a plus for uncertainties. If you are not sure how much of an income to provide, try looking for something that provides 70-80% of your current Pre-Retirement Income (This number will vary depending on what type of lifestyle you leave)

- Set Short and Long- Term Financial Goals

Short-term goals could be a high-interest savings account or saving for retirement holidays that you will want in early retirement. Your long-term goals may be estate planning, making charitable contributions, or the financial support of people you want to take care of when you are gone.

Write Your Financial Goals… If you write down your financial goals and commit to them as though they were part of the Ten Commandments, it may be like a written vision for what must be accomplished so that retirement includes doing precisely those things burning in your soul. These targets' financial goals have a preventive purpose, allowing us to realize our projects without dreaming too much and acting with good ownership over the issues.

Step 4: Create a Map to Success

Now that you have a few personal and financial goals, let me tie them together with a roadmap. Consider this a strategic but flexible plan to bring you one step closer to your retirement vision.

- Divide Goals into Manageable Tasks

Maybe one of your goals is to downsize… something you can immediately do about it may be decluttering or looking at real estate nearby. For our travel goals, consider the countries you would like to visit and plan how many times a year you wish to go—making those big goals more achievable and less daunting but breaking them down into small steps.

- Prioritize Your Goals

However, other goals could feel more urgent or time-specific. For example, health goals may be considered more important than picking up a new hobby. You will know where your focus should be to spend most of your time and money.

- Set Milestones

A way to look at milestones is just as signposts on the journey. If, for example, your vision is related to learning how to paint, a milestone would be stepping towards it, either enlisting in a painting class or finishing the first piece of art. This makes you excited and happy to keep going by reaching these milestones.

- Review and Adjust Regularly

Your goals may change as life brings new experiences. Try to review your roadmap once (or twice) a year. This allows you time to review, refocus, and continue on the path toward retirement.

Step 5: Seeing the success

Visualization is a paramount tool for securing the retirement of your vision. That is not just hot air; research supports the idea that those who can visualize our victory are more likely to attain it. Close your eyes and visualize retirement for you down to the last detail. Imagine sitting on your balcony and having tea in the morning, walking around new city streets, or laughing with family members during holidays. Make this visualization vivid or abstract and lush, using the sounds and sensations of each scene.

Vision Board: If you are a visual guy, make a vision board. Cut out pictures and make a picture board with words or images of what you want from your retirement. Put this board somewhere you can see it every day to remind yourself of the kind of life that you're working towards.

Turning Vision into Reality

Consistently taking action on impactful steps will manifest your vision. As you will recall, retirement is neither a place nor an outcome. It is an opportunity to practice living out the life you have designed. Creating and initiating a target retirement vision is not something you can complete in one day—it develops into layers over time. Allow your vision to grow and change as you get clear on what is essential in life.

CHAPTER 2

How to Calculate your Retirement Number

For some, retirement seems like a far-off dream; for others, it's close. Knowing your financial "retirement number" is vital to a happy, stress-free retirement. Well, what is this number, and how do we get it? Calculating your retirement number can arrive at a lump sum that should cover one's living expenses for however long you expect to be retired and not in the labor force. It's your retirement plan's bedrock! It will allow you to wrap your head around this figure and then relax, knowing everything is set for a great retirement. Identifying your retirement number might seem daunting, but I will show you a simple 3-step process to get started. We will work through the factors determining this number, including lifestyle, healthcare needs, inflation, and what types of income streams you might expect in retirement.

Step 1: Estimate Your Retirement Costs

First, you need to know your retirement number and figure out (or at least have a general sense of) what your monthly expenses will be like in retirement. Consider this your baseline financial base: things you know are coming every month but don't change. It's important to estimate these costs as accurately as possible since they will be part of your retirement budget.

Below is a list of general categories to consider:

- Housing

Feel free to visit *https://creditrepair.xyz/cd-reviews.html*, to see a list of frequently wanted housing expenses, including mortgage payments, rent and property taxes, and homeowners' insurance—and don't forget maintenance costs are the most typical expenses here. Even if you pay off your home by retirement, ongoing costs like taxes and maintenance don't go away, and maybe even association fees if you're in a community setting.

- Medical

As this sector is usually challenging to predict but can never wholly be missed. While Medicare covers some misfortunes, you may have to pay premiums, co-pays, and prescription medicinal drugs. Consider long-term care (e.g., home health or assisted living).

- Food

Utilities to Home and Transport, etc. You may not have to worry about transportation expenses if you aren't commuting as frequently anymore, but keep in mind that your mode of transport might change, or you could increase the amount spent on mobility.

- Fun and Travel

You may also imagine some travel during retirement (or spending more time on things you love to do). Remember, retirement is your turning point in life, and it should be the time to live what you might want to spend here...

- Unexpected Expenses

Plan for unexpected events like home repairs, car breakdowns, or other unplanned costs. Several financial advisors suggest reserving 10–15% of your overall expenditures for this. Once you have calculated these expenses, add them to an annual total. Note that this should not be concrete, as your needs may change. But being vigilant and maintaining a robust underpinning means you will never be blindsided.

Step 2: Consider longevity and inflation

Next is the duration of retirement, or how long you plan to retire. We cannot predict with certainty how long we will live, but a conservative longevity estimate should keep you from underestimating your retirement savings needs. Most people anticipate somewhere around 25-30 years of no income stream from their job (assuming they retire around age 65). And if you foresee a more extended life ahead, maybe even stretch that out to 100 years or so.

And then there's inflation. While modest inflation can help protect your buying power, higher rates of this economic challenge will surely eat into the purchasing power so specific to an early retirement lifestyle, and you should plan accordingly. This can significantly change your central estimate, even if you take a conservative 2-3% annual inflation rate. Planning for Inflation – Make sure your retirement income adapts to rising costs and doesn't leave you short of funds later on down the track like many retirees face when they run out of money in their 80s or beyond.

Step 3: Calculate Your Retirement Number

So, after we have sold for your annual costs and accounted for longevity risk and inflation, let us calculate how much money you need to retire! The idea is to have a pot of money that can sustainably fund your lifestyle without being depleted.

A common rule of thumb is the 4% rule: this guideline stipulates that you should not withdraw more than 4% each year from your retirement portfolio. Applying this rule, you can calculate your expected retirement number by multiplying 25 by the total value you usually spend annually. For instance, if you think $50,000 per year will be needed to support everyday living expenses, it should total at least 1.25 million dollars saved (excluding pensions).

Here's the formula:

Annual Expenses x 25 (Retirement Number)

And keep in mind that this will be your starting place—bear in mind that it's a rough ballpark. A 3% or even a 3.5% withdrawal rate provides more cushion, so that might be your choice instead if you take the conservative approach to safe withdrawals (and, therefore, raises the amount of savings needed).

Step 4: Evaluate and Optimize Your Savings and Investments

After you find your target retirement number, the next step is to look at savings and investments to determine how far you are from achieving it. The primary types of assets that will assure your accompanying them in retirement can be classified as:

- Retirement Accounts

401(k)s, IRAs, and other tax-advantaged accounts. Many of these will enable your investment to develop free of tax, making them a fantastic vehicle for retirement cost savings. Take a look at A) how much you have saved in these accounts and B) what that money will likely grow into overtime (including contributions, employer matches [if applicable], and the excellent voodoo magic known as market performance).

- Social Security

If you will be in the U.S., Social Security is probably part of your retirement income. Depending on your earnings history, the age at which you begin to receive benefits determines the percentage of your monthly stated benefit. The problem with these statistics is that waiting until age 70 to claim Social Security can increase the size of your check. Still, everyone's financial situation is different, and it's essential to plan accordingly.

- Pensions

This is a formidable and steady income stream if you have one from an employer. Find Out the Fine Print -How long do the benefits last?-Do they increase with inflation? Beyond retirement accounts, taxable investment accounts provide another source of income. Although you will want to think about taxes on gains, these accounts are one of the ways that help with some withdrawal options compared to traditional retirement accounts.

- Annuities

Some purchase an annuity to provide guaranteed income in retirement. While an annuity can be an excellent way to provide regular income, you must be aware of the limitations or stipulations, fees, and payouts.

- Real Estate/Other Passive Income Sources

If you have rental property or some other source of passive income, this could be a smart way to add cushioning to your retirement savings. Calculate your revenue from these sources, considering possible changes in the market and maintenance.

Step 5: Finding Retirement Income Streams

Besides your saving scheme, you may also want to consider different ways of generating money, which is a great way to hold on to other aspects when the mainstream option offers thin. Try some of the following options:

- Work part-time or Consult:

Other retirees work in the same area for at least some time. It is one way to make some pocket money and stay engaged. Besides, you can also improve with a schedule that suits your life.

- Dividend and Interest Income

If you receive dividends on stock, bonds, or interest from savings accounts, you regularly receive income at a predictable level. However, the expected returns may vary with market conditions, so it's better to spread them thin over various income-producing assets.

- Sell Assets or Downsize:

Selling your home or other assets may be another strategy for adding money to your retirement accounts. For example, selling your current home and downsizing might give you cash to use elsewhere for expenses or investments.

- Health Savings Accounts (HSAs):

If you have been saving in an HSA, this makes and provides a tax-deductible way to pay for health care expenses. Since they are tax-free, HSAs are a money-saving way to pay for health care.

- Reverse Mortgage

Homeowners can take on a reverse mortgage…Trading home equity for cash while living in your home without selling it. A side note: This is not for everyone, or it may be difficult if you only have your home as an asset to work with.

- Monitoring your progress and make and Adjustments:

After you determine your retirement number and start evaluating what resources you have to work with, it's essential to monitor how things are going. Retirement planning is not a once-and-done thing. Whether it be life events, economic changes, or your ambitions, you may change how you save.

Some tips for staying on track:

Annual Check-Ins: Review your retirement accounts and income streams to see where you are concerning achieving your number. In time, said minor adaptations could serve as the heralds of greater ones.

Diversification and Risk Management: Many investors look to diversify investments in retirement for risk reduction. As you near retirement, many people move out of stocks and into bonds or other less volatile investments- decreasing the impact on your portfolio as bond yields rise.

An emergency fund: You should have an emergency savings reserve to pay for unexpected bills. You can avoid dipping into your retirement funds to cover surprise expenses this way.

CHAPTER 3

Budgeting for the Long Haul

Planning for retirement is like planning to take a long car vacation; the trip may go wonderfully, but there will always be some bumps in the road and unexpected detours. A budget is a classic map plotting a direct course on how you might navigate this wild world by identifying/allocating both the known and unknown essentials. A thoughtful budget enables you to live the life important for being concerned with not saving your money too soon! Let's examine how to budget money for big-picture financial planning over the long haul, including retirement expenses, without going broke. It is more than just counting pennies; it is about knowing where your money goes, what future costs may arise, and making strategic decisions that align with your priorities. Because…you are meant to enjoy retirement, not be a slave.

Step 1: Approximate Your Monthly and Annual Expenses

1. Know your expenses (monthly and yearly) into retirement. Most of us are probably in for a change regarding these costs. For example, you could spend less on commuting and workwear but more on healthcare or leisure. Even when you are mortgage-free, housing contributes to one of the highest costs during retirement. In addition to the mortgage, you have property taxes, homeowners insurance, utilities, maintenance, and perhaps HOA fees (if it's a way of life where yard work is someone else's headache).

Rent/Mortgage: This will likely be your most significant monthly expense if you rent or pay a mortgage. The pros: This is a pre-retirement cost-benefit tax return as a retiree division, creating the necessary barrier.

Property Taxes and insurance are hard to predict. Property values may be increasing rapidly in many areas, so these costs might buy you more houses later, while elsewhere, they will rise.

Upkeep: Remember to save money for maintenance and repairs, which will eventually add up.

2. Healthcare / Medical Costs:

Health expenses can range from next-to-nothing to six figures, depending on your health needs and location, as well as the extent of insurance coverage you have. Although Medicare covers some of these costs, there are still going to be out-of-pocket expenses

Insurance Premiums: You may need to pay monthly premiums for Medicare and supplemental insurance policies, such as Medigap or a private health plan. Be sure not to include those on your pricing model.

Expanded details: This will show you a breakdown of your out-of-pocket costs (e.g., co-pays, deductibles, and whatever else wasn't covered by insurance) for medical services or medications, etc. Those costs might increase, mainly as healthcare needs grow.

Long-Term Care: Most of us will never need long-term care, but it won't kill you to plan for the possibility. Since long-term care is an issue, prepare by purchasing LTC insurance or self-insuring for possible assisted living and nursing home expenses.

3. Daily Living Expenses:

Daily costs such as groceries, transportation, and utilities will still be part of your budget in retirement. Yes, some spending may be down," but you still need to know that number.

Food and Household Supplies: There are no work lunches or as much shopping for a large family. You might spend slightly less on food now than before; however, retirement can also bring additional social dining, which makes up the difference with friends on lunch dates, talk coffee groups, etc., at least once per week, of course!

Transportation: You might not have to spend as much on commuting, but similarly, plan for the maintenance of your vehicle and insurance or even rideshare/public transportation.

Utilities and Communication: (This constitutes your electricity, water, internet bill, and phone service.) Utilities could be slightly lower depending on whether you live in a smaller or less energy-consuming space.

4. Leisure and Hobbies:

You are most certainly due to living a life of fun after retirement, but leisure activities can be expensive. Whether golf, travel, or crafting, save money for what you love doing.

Travel and Vacations: Retirement is frequently seen as a time to travel, and regardless of whether that means an annual family trip or places you want to see before your chop can be set on any butcher block chopping board, those costs should now also likewise fill in the budget for retirement.

Hobbies and Classes: Retirement is an excellent time to enjoy hobbies, but will supplies, equipment, and classes take money from your budget?

5. Hidden and Surprising Expenses:

Allocate a bit of your budget for these because should something go wrong with the project, you want to have money stashed away. Sometimes, life gets in the way, and unexpected home repairs, medical needs, or family emergencies pop up.

Emergency Fund: To not break your budget to pieces whenever there are expenses you cannot entirely anticipate, having an emergency fund can save you a lot by keeping all of the sudden expenditures within it.

Donations and Charities: From gifting to family members or giving contributions to worthy causes, many retirees find joy in helping others. Having little allowance for these gestures can contribute to your strength of giving.

Tips for Sustainable Living

Well, Budgeting starts with it. Sustaining it over time takes some work, and we use a few tricks to ensure those resources stretch far down the road. Check our practical tips below to ensure you do everything possible to get your money through retirement and sustainable living.

1. Monitor Your Spending and Adapt as Necessary

After you have a budget, monitor how closely your actual spending matches what you said it would be. Monitor your spending for at least a couple of years to ensure you have built-in enough leeway in the rate-of-return estimates, especially with high-frequency periodic checking of categories exceeding expectations regarding early retirement. From this little equation, you realize that changes might be needed as your lifestyle shifts or evolves, and thus, thoughtful planning can avoid situations structured to make someone incur more significant money problems down the road.

2. Embrace a Flexible Budget

And that is the beauty of retirement — it puts you in charge. Specific bills, like healthcare, are less controllable in price than others, but you can make up the difference elsewhere. For example, if you use more money than anticipated on travel in one year, try to balance your budget by pulling funds from a less critical category or putting off more significant purchases. The ability to change your lifestyle without sacrificing the overall quality of life.

3. Check Out Senior Discounts and Benefits

Retiring has its advantages — not least of all, discounts for seniors. Discounts for Retirees: Many businesses, from restaurants to travel companies, offer discounts specifically for retirees. These perks can add to significant savings, so ask about them everywhere. These include programs such as savings on phone, internet, and other bills specifically for retirees.

4. Move or Downsize if Needed

Downsizing is an obvious route to save money, especially if you own a large home or property. Selling your big family home to a smaller, more manageable place can reduce property taxes, maintenance, and utilities. Others may relocate to cheaper housing areas or states known for friendly pension tax policy rehabilitation. Moving is no small decision, but it may help logistically and financially if that move closely aligns with your mission.

5. Stay Active and Healthy

Although it does not seem like a financial tip, being physically active and healthy has substantial long-term effects on your financial situation. Because healthcare is a considerable expense when retired, better health can spent on preventive care, which even leads to lower costs for exercise and healthy food. It also invests in your quality of life to connect you and give you the best retirement experience.

6. Set Financial Boundaries

Even as a retiree, friends or family may try to siphon funds from you if they know money is saved in your nest egg. While generosity is excellent, giving freely with no limits can end your retirement. It is difficult to say no, but by doing so, you become the only one who keeps your personal and financial stability on its feet and sees a good life without having too much weight on other things.

7. Automate Payments and Savings

Enlist your utilities, investments, and fun money to pay themselves automatically. Automation also streamlines your budget, which lessens the chances of late payment or spending more than you have. Retirees can automate a "fun fund" to set aside money for entertainment and recreation without dipping into long-term savings.

Balancing Spending and Saving

Budgeting doesn't mean eliminating; it means balancing enjoying your retirement and ensuring you don't outlive the money. Here are a few ways to achieve this balance.

The 50-30-20 Rule: This rule is one of the most common budgeting methods; it suggests putting some spending into needs- (about half), wants (around a third), or savings at twenty percent. In retirement, this can be a helpful rule of thumb with appropriate adjustments as necessary. As another example, you may also want to bias your spending towards the "wants" in early retirement since you will likely be most active.

Plan for Go-Go, Slow-Go, No-G0 Phases— Many finance experts often talk about the three phases of retirement: go-go years (active), slow-go years (still moving but a little slower and less active), and no-g0s, which are all about health-focused work around the house. Because you will spend differently in each phase, identifying your stage can help you adjust your spending appropriately.

Focus on Experiences, Not Stuff: In retirement, experiences (traveling, doing hobbies) can be more valuable than buying stuff. Even if you have always been an average-income or lower-middle-class person, your experiences can be more prosperous and full of life than those of wealthy people who live their lives surrounded by only the finest material things.

Set up a Guilt-Free Fund: Set aside an amount you can afford from your regular budget to spend on whatever makes you happy. This fund is a great way to indulge periodically, whether for going out with friends, to dinner, to movies, or purchasing something special, without throwing your overall financial plan off track.

Budgeting is not so easy, but it is one of the most exciting parts of retirement planning. You can enjoy retirement and never have to worry about money just as long as you know precisely what those outflows are and how well under control they remain. CODE: A responsible budget does not constrain your lifestyle; it enables it.

Chapter 4

Investment Strategies for Security

How you invest can change significantly as retirement draws near — or after it has already started. In retirement, busting out huge returns is only for the reckless as stability becomes paramount. Low-risk investments provide security and, at the same time, a little growth, so you can protect what you have saved and create regular income streams that you can leverage for years. This chapter will discuss some low-risk investments recommended for retirees, and we have even more tips on adjusting your portfolio below. In short, let's keep it basic and wise and follow what is vital—creating a viable strategy that allows you to sleep well at night and breathe easily.

Why Low-Risk Investments?

Before we discuss the different types of investments in detail, let me explain why retirees must have access to low-risk investing. In the early parts of your career, you probably were more aggressive with investing. When you had time and could ride out market swings, it made sense to put growth-oriented assets like stocks in a portfolio because downturns were temporary—the world bounced back. In retirement, however, the emphasis will move away from growth and stability.

That nest egg is often the result of years or decades of hard work, and well... you want to protect that sucker! These investments provide a steady and more secure return, ensuring you won't wake up one morning with market-shattering news, resulting in most of your savings disappearing.

Investment of any type comes with research with comments on a risk level, namely that it never entirely goes to zero; however, there are options where some stability while modest growth might also be possible. This balance keeps your retirement savings from running out before you do so.

Six Low-Risk Investments for Retirees

Here are some of the best low-risk investment options for retirees: The returns on each investment are different, and combining them for a more diversified strategy is usually best.

1. High-Yield Savings Accounts/Certificates of Deposits CDs

High-yield savings accounts or certificates of deposit (CDs) are among the most accessible, secure places to store reserves. Bank CDs. These are FDIC-insured (which means your principal is protected, but you should check on any limits) and offer a rate that does not change.

- High-Yield Savings Accounts:

A high-yielding savings account can come with a higher interest rate than standard saving accounts and is usually more liquid (so you won't need too much notice to access the money.)

- Certificates of Deposit (CDs):

CDs tie up your money for a few months or several years and pay higher interest rates than ordinary savings accounts. Just make sure, however, that CDs usually have early withdrawal penalties, so you might be better off putting money there only for funds you won't need shortly. Both are good options for an emergency fund or anything else you might need that money for in the next five to ten years.

2. Bonds and Bond Funds

Many retirees use Bonds as a traditional safe investment for predictable and regular income. Locking the money in for a certain period because you owe it to a government or corporation is called "buying bonds" and agreeing that they will pay back some interest like monthly. Generally, bonds are less volatile than stocks and are therefore considered the safer play, but there is some nuance.

- Government Bonds

These are IOUs that the government issues, as well as U.S. Treasury bonds, bills, and notes—take your pick! Because they are backed by the big wrong US Government that has everybody's better interests at heart, they tend to be considered some of the safest investments. Treasury Inflation-Protected Securities (TIPS) are also more common since they safeguard against inflation.

- Municipal Bonds:

Different states and municipalities offer tax-free interest on these bonds, which can be very appealing if you pay taxes in a high bracket. But again, municipal bonds are not all equal, and evaluating the issuer's creditworthiness is essential.

- Corporate Bonds[18]:

Bonds issued by reputable corporations that provide higher yields than government bonds but are less stable. Stick with high-quality "investment-grade" bonds issued by well-regarded companies to limit risk.

3. Bond Funds and ETFs

If you choose not to select individual bonds, bond funds, or an exchange-traded fund (ETF) that pools several different types of bonds, it can be worth considering. All offer diversification and professional management to spread risk over multiple bonds. Either way, you must be vigilant of fees that could reduce returns.

4. Dividend-Paying Stocks

While stocks tend to be riskier than bonds, some make great retirement investments, especially dividend-paying ones.

These usually involve creating income-giving securities by buying shares in companies with well-established reputations that pay regular dividends to shareholders. Examples include many utilities, healthcare companies, and consumer goods companies. In the long term, dividend-paying stocks eventually deliver earnings through dividends and go up quite fast compared to other low & no-dividend-paying growth stocks. Nevertheless, opt for stable blue chips with a track record of regular dividend payouts. You can also diversify your income stream by investing in dividend-focused ETFs or mutual funds that hold positions across multiple companies.

5. Annuities

An annuity is a financial product that provides continuous payments, often for the remainder of your life. You buy an annuity in which the insurance company (annuitant) offers to pay out a set amount every month for life or until the end of an agreed-upon time frame, like 15 years. Immediate Annuities pay income soon after you invest, and they can be a solid option if you want to turn some of your savings into steady payments.

Fixed Annuities: Fixed annuities pay certified interest rate returns during a fixed timeframe, offering one more excellent value if the person seeks income stability. Unlike variable annuities, these plans do not change with the market.

These are complex products with associated fees, and it makes sense to get help if you opt for one. They may provide some peace of mind and help protect against running out of money, but it's essential to understand their terms and fee structures fully.

6. Investment Trusts, or REITs

Invest in property indirectly via the stock market. If you want to hit the real estate types above but it is too much of a hassle for direct ownership, Real Estate Investment Trusts (REITs) offer an acquisition way to invest your money into join. Such companies are also known as real estate investment trusts (REITs), and they must pay out at least 90% of their net income to shareholders in the form of dividends by law.

REITs are great for income and typically offer higher yields than traditional dividend stocks, although with more volatility. They give you real estate exposure without having to manage an individual property, and they are perfect if you are looking for a diversified instead of income-producing investment.

How to Balance your Portfolio for Retirement

Now that you know how low-risk investments work, let's see where they fit in your portfolio. Below are a few things you can do to shift your investment holdings appropriate for the income and stability focus typical of retirement.

- Focus on Income-Generating Assets

Once retired, growth is not as significant as income. These assets become "retirement paychecks" because they can help you keep your lifestyle but defer the principal to later retirement when inflation is lower and returns may be higher.

- Diversify to Low-Risk Assets

Diversification shouldn't just be a lost concept in retirement. Diversify across the lower-risk avenues to reduce dependence on any one source of investment. A combination of bonds, stocks that pay dividends, and other conservative investments can provide income without going into capital preservation overdrive. Diversifying would mean you are much better positioned to deal with any instability linked within specific markets or sectors.

- Apply Inflation Protection Merhods

Because inflation can destroy your purchasing power over time, it is essential to have some inflation-protected assets. Treasury Inflation-Protected Securities (TIPS) is a sound place to start here, as is with dividend-paying stocks that have long since upped their payouts, often counterbalancing escalating prices.

- Rebalance Periodically

Similarly, when you are in retirement, you must rebalance your portfolio regularly so that the state of your investments never gets too far from where they ought to be given what you want those assets for. Market changes can mean your asset allocation may shift and more (or less) of some assets than you planned. A periodic review (perhaps annually or semi-annually) can maintain your portfolio.

- Build a Cash Reserve

A cash reserve can be used for short-term needs and provide a cushion so you do not have to sell investments during market declines. This is a prudent approach as well and would typically allow you to have 1-2 years of living expenses in something more readily accessible, such as your emergency fund (in a high-yield savings account or money market) so that the funds are available for emergencies without selling long-term growth assets. After all, your investments should underpin the lifestyle you have worked so hard for. So, as we adapt and tweak our plan, you can always fall back on your peace of mind—the real purpose of all this is to have less stress about money when someone else is managing yours so you can enjoy retirement.

CHAPTER 5

Monthly Income Planning Strategy

What will I have to live on each month when it comes time for retirement? Going from a steady paycheck for years... to retirement is quite an adjustment. A secure retirement is all about creating a predictable income strategy that will serve you well throughout your golden years and work in concert with the lifestyle goals and spending plan you have mapped out. In this chapter, I will bring you the basics of putting together a monthly income strategy that seamlessly incorporates different sources of earnings into your life. We will unpack the basics of passive vs active income streams and dive even further into how to improve each one so that they can keep your financial life afloat while still enjoying all of those retired freedoms.

How to Find Your Income Needs

So, before we move on to some detailed income strategy options, you must know your monthly expenses—those basic living expenses like housing, food, healthcare, and utilities—and those proverbial "whatever" costs (travel, hobbies, or something unexpected). Knowing exactly how much (and where) your money is going enables you to draw up an income plan that isn't too tight nor too risk-averse.

1. After calculating what you need to set aside for monthly expenses, add a cushion if possible in case of unplanned needs like home repairs or medical bills. I suggest allocating 10–15% over your costs to ensure you have some cushion for unforeseen surprises. That way, you won't be tempted to raid your retirement savings early.

2. Determining Funding Streams

There are many ways to generate retirement income; typically, the best route is a combination of two or more strategies. This blog post outlines the six income streams and, most importantly, how we can fit them into our monthly plan.

- Social Security

This then becomes the foundation from which most retirees draw their retirement income. What You Get: The payment is based on your earning history and when you choose to start collecting benefits. For example, the longer you delay claiming Social Security (up until age 70), the more significant your monthly benefit.

Consider your general health, expected lifespan, and other income streams before claiming social security. Delaying benefits gives you a more extensive monthly check when you are older, which could help with rising inflation and unexpected expenses. However, there may be a case of claiming benefits earlier if you have little other income.

- Pension Income

Suppose you are lucky enough to have a pension generated by your employer that is meaningful income. It is essential to study your plan because pension plans can differ in the benefits paid and how they are collected. While some pension plans are structured for lump-sum payments, others pay monthly benefits to recipients over their lifetimes. Whether you should elect a lump sum or an annuity is another nagging question you may have — but if this decision pertains to your health, other income, and ready ability to handle money wisely (or not), the determination rests with personal factors.

- change into Retirement Accounts (401(k), IRA, Roth IRA)

Most of your income will likely come from retirement accounts. With traditional accounts — 401(k)s and IRAs, for example — you must start taking required minimum distributions (RMDs) by age 72. Nevertheless, Roth IRAs are not subject to RMDs, making them an ideal income planning tool.

For most retirees, withdrawing from traditional accounts should be done first to satisfy RMDs while leaving Roth account withdrawals for later years. This strategy allows you to access money for the immediate tax bill, and DURING WHILE THE SECURE Act changed when Guardian must take an RMD from inherited IRAs that came into effect on 1/01/20, funds remain in a Roth account where they can continue growing (TAX-FREE) as long as possible.

- Dividends and Interest Income

Buying shares that pay timely dividends, bonds, and other income-generating assets gives a regular cash flow. Interest on bonds vs. dividends on dividend stocks (shares of companies that re-distribute some portion of earnings to shareholders). Although not entirely without risk, these investments are valuable to your retirement plan income.

You may want to consider a dividend-focused or bond fund that can provide extra diversification and reduced risk than a getting older available-for-purchase market. Remember that housing can have its hiccups depending on snowflakes ……. so ensure you are comfortable with the risk profile of any investments here

- Annuities

An annuity is a financial product that can give you an income stream – generally assured. You provide an annuity provider a chunk of cash, and they pay you back in regular installments or for your entire lifetime. Annuities are typically complex and often come with various fees, so know what you're buying. With fixed annuities, you are paid a predictable amount, and with variable annuities, you receive an amount based on your portfolio's performance.

If you need a consistent income and can live with your money being tied up, an annuity could make sense for some of the funds in your portfolio.

- Part-Time Work or Consulting

You may have retired from full-time employment, but many retirees can earn at least some income or perhaps even find purpose in part-time work or consulting. It's a great way to keep active and earn extra retirement money. When you freelance or consult, you can work whenever you please and set whatever hourly rate works best for your lifestyle.

Wow, What a simple task.

Balancing Passive and Active Income

Having discussed potential income streams, let us focus on balancing active and passive forms of income. You don't have to work for income, such as Social Security retirement payments, pensions, or investments in stocks that pay dividends. Invoke Later Meanwhile, active income is generated by part-time jobs or any other types of continued exertion. In retirement, you should (ideally) have more passive income than when working because it gives you greater security and allows for not working.

Active income can help cover additional costs or challenging spending opportunities, but it should be like for. [ETS1] A mix between passive and active income provides the benefit of hybrid income, which allows you to have financial return with freedom for retirement instead of being consumed by gains only.

Also, Develop a Monthly Income Approach: Now, let's combine it all into a monthly income strategy. This plan considers your current capital needs while also considering long-term savings.

1. Establish a Baseline Income

Start by listing your guaranteed income sources: Social Security (if applicable), pensions, and all annuities. This is your baseline, the surface of everything. It should include all necessities: housing, healthcare, food, and whatever else you need to live daily (transportation? It depends). Having a baseline income to cover the essentials regardless of what happens is comforting.

2. Layer in Supplemental Income

Then, do these part-time and work-from-home stints to pay your compound discretionary costs. This can be retirement account withdrawals, dividends, or any income from part-time work. You can add extra income to your base, allowing you to pay for travel or hobbies / eating out without fear of not covering all things essential.

3. Fixed Withdrawal Rates for Retirement Accounts

Following a safe withdrawal rate for your 401k or IRA is crucial in retirement. The 4% rule, a popular guideline for retirement spending, suggests that you withdraw 4% of your savings each year so the money does not run out. However, in less specific markets, few retirees are comfortable with that and prefer to use something closer to 3% (or maybe even as low as 3-31/2%) for an essential dose of security.

While this is a solid pace, it's not the 100% correct rate. How much will that pay you? That depends on your health, lifestyle, and market conditions.

4. Automate Monthly Withdrawals

Automating your withdrawals simplifies the process, and you can think of it less like a withdrawal plan and more like a "paycheck" that comes bright and early every month. Some financial institutions permit the transfer via a monthly withdrawal from your retirement account(s) directly into your checking. This aids in ensuring you are not overspending while keeping your cash flow consistent and steady.

5. Maintain an Emergency Fund

While you may have a good income plan in place, there will still probably be things that come up."]; Make sure to have at least 6-12 months of your expenses in an emergency fund. You can use this reserve for any unforeseen circumstances, and it will not force you to touch anything long-term. A high-yield savings account is a beautiful spot to park these funds, ready for you in case of an emergency while still being somewhat rewarded.

How to Properly Manager your Income

After having a passive income method, the next thing you have to do is continue focusing on that revenue approach. We must deal with this because we know that one day, you will retire. So here are ways to manage income properly and maintain a solid financial position through retirement.

- Develop a Habit of Reviewing Your Strategy

Review your income plan at least once a year. Circumstances in life, conditions on the market, and a person's goals can also change. Reviewing your plan helps you keep up with changes in what matters and allows you to adjust as needed.

- Keep Taxes in Mind

Just because you retire doesn't mean the taxes go away, so it's important to factor them in from this effect. Income from traditional retirement accounts, dividends, and Social Security benefits are taxable. Reducing your tax burden with some planned, tax-efficient strategies — pulling from Roth accounts last (if you have them) or spreading out those withdrawals. Discuss your specific needs with a financial planner or tax advisor.

- Avoid spending too much

Retirees typically pay more in the initial years of retirement, primarily on traveling and skills. To enjoy retirement, it is necessary to control spending and beware of funds reaching an end. Adding five provision years once an individual reaches age thirty means building a discretionary allowance for these years — without shooting past your ultimate goals.

- Be Flexible About Your Withdrawal Rates

Withdrawal rates: As noted, withdrawal levels might have to be scaled back. When the market is strong, you can push your rate up a little, but it always pays to give yourself some slack in slower years. Not only will making withdrawals easier prevent your capital from being eroded, but it should also protect upstream income over time.

CHAPTER 6

Healthcare and Insurance Planning

One of the most significant parts of retirement planning is healthcare. The older we get, the more healthcare we need; therefore, insurance coverage becomes important. Medicare pays certain costs for most Americans aged 65 or older. However, Medicare doesn't cover everything, and many retirees will find that supplemental insurance such as Medigap or a Medicare Advantage plan can be crucial to filling in the gaps of traditional coverage. This chapter covers the ingredients of Medicare—Supplemental insurance options—And how to prepare for surprise medical bills. Knowing these components will help protect you against the cost of healthcare in retirement so they do not catch you by surprise.

Medicare

Medicare is a federal health insurance program for people 65 and older, as well as for under-65 persons who have been disabled) Because Medicare comes in multiple parts, each focusing on different types of care, knowing the ins and outs is vital to charting your course.

Step 1. Medicare Part A (Hospital Insurance)

Medicare has two parts. Part A covers hospital treatment, including inpatient stays, care at a skilled nursing facility, hospice care, and some home health care. You Pay a Premium for Part A. Most people cannot pay any monthly premium if they or their spouse paid Medicare taxes while working for at least 10 years. However, it is essential to note that there are deductibles and coinsurance costs for hospital stays.

Deductible (2024): $1,632 for each benefit period. This applies to the first 60 days of an inpatient hospital stay.

Coinsurance: After 60 days, you pay coinsurance for covered services. These amounts change annually, so go to www.Medicare.gov/your-medicare-costs for the current numbers.

Step 2. Medicare (Medical Insurance)

Part B includes coverage for outpatient care, doctor visits, preventative services, and some parts of home health care. Yes, unlike Part A, which you have already paid with a payroll tax deduction, Part B is a premium that is taken out of your monthly benefits when calculated based on on-come decisions.

The Standard Part B monthly premium for 2024 is $174.70 (unchanged from the amount announced in June).

Deductible and Coinsurance: in 2024, deductibles for Part B are $240 per year. Once you meet this deductible, you pay 20% of the Medicare-approved amount for most doctor services, outpatient therapy, and durable medical equipment.

Step 3. Medicare Part C (also known as Medicare Advantage)

These plans are available for you after being approved by Medicare, and they are called a medicare advantage plan (part C) offered by some private insurance companies. These plans cover parts A & B plus extra dental, vision, and hearing benefits. This can be convenient because many Advantage plans also include prescription drug coverage.

Cost of Medicare Advantage: Premiums vary based on plan and location. Other plans have no premiums but may have higher out-of-pocket costs or only cover care from select networks. Picking an Advantage Plan, It is important to double-check whether your regular doctors participate in a particular Medicare Advance plan so that you can be sure they will still care for you.

Step 4. This includes Medicare Part D (prescription drug coverage)

Part D/Medicare provides prescription drug coverage, which is critical for many seniors. Private insurers also offer Part D plans, and like Medicare Advantage, their premiums (and to a much greater extent) out-of-pocket costs can vary widely.

With the Part D drug plan national base beneficiary premium of about $35.50/month in 2024, premiums can still vary by both plan and location;

Deductibles & Copays: Part D plans have deductibles and require paying a copay or coinsurance on each prescription. There is also a "donut hole," where coverage falls off due to high costs exceeding the spending threshold, but full catastrophic coverage will take effect and cover higher expenses.

Insurance policies you can sign up for on the side

Because Medicare does not cover all healthcare costs, many retirees turn to supplemental insurance to help cope with out-of-pocket expenses. Dive into some of the top variants below, along with their explanation.

1. Medigap (list of Medicare Supplement Insurance)

These Medigap plans (provided by private insurance companies) help pick up where original Medicare leaves off — paying some shared costs like copays, coinsurance, and deductibles. Medigap is a standardized policy in which each plan gets identified by the letter (e.g., Plan G, N) offering different coverage.

These Medigap plans differ in what they cover. For instance, Plan G pays for Part A and B copays, the Part A deductible (high), and out-of-country urgent care expenses.

Many seniors are drawn to these policies by their low premiums. While the potential savings exist, even a relatively modest $100 monthly payment can soar past $300 per month, depending on location and plan. Although an added expense, Medigap coverage can be worth the peace of mind it may bring by protecting you from some costly medical surprises. You should know you cannot have a Medicare Advantage or Medigap Plan; it is either an or

2. Medicare Advantage Plans

First, as I said to earlier, Medicare Advantage plans usually offer extra benefits on top of the ones already covered by Original Medicare. If you suffer from Original Medicare and Medigap, these plans may provide an alternative for supplementary benefits like dental with vision. However, remember that Advantage plans usually have more excellent provider and network restrictions than original Medicare plans, so if you would like more flexibility with your care, Medigap might be a better option.

3. Long-Term Care Insurance

Medicare does not cover long-term care (help with day-to-day activities or care in a nursing home). Long-term care insurance can be a valuable tool for covering these expenses, which may be hefty. No national policy and significant variations in the care covered and benefits provided exist.

Long-Term Care Insurance: While premiums can be pricey and often increase as you age (so it's typically better to look into options while younger), this is one way some Americans pay for LTC.

Other Choices: Hybrid policies that offer a blend of life insurance with long-term coverage or cash earmarked for LTC costs are options some retired people consider.

Long-term care insurance is not for everyone, but it may be an option you want to explore if guarding your savings against the leading long-term care expenses is a priority. Including Unforeseen Medical Expenses in Your Budget

Most retirees face surprise health care bills. Out-of-Pocket Costs — Medicare and supplemental insurance will likely reduce your expenses, but you probably have them.

How to Budget and Plan Your Expenses.

1. Create an HSA (Health Savings Account)

Another consideration for people still working and accessing a high-deductible health plan is contributing to an HSA (Health Savings Account). An HSA has triple tax advantages: contributions are pre-tax (a deduction reduces your income and therefore lowers the taxes you owe), earnings grow without taxing, and qualified medical expenses that have nothing to do with retirement can be taken out for free. Using Your HSA in Retirement: You can use the money for anything after age 65 (though non-medical withdrawals are still taxed). That being said, the more health you have, the more freedom you have to use your HSA funds for any healthcare cost, maximizing its benefit.

2. Establish a Health-Related Contingency Fund

You can broaden and save better by adding separate funds to your emergency fund for an unanticipated ailment. This distinct reserve is intended to help you meet high deductibles, cost-sharing requirements, or care that Medicare doesn't cover. The average individual should strive to have at least several months of healthcare expenses saved up (including copays, deductibles, and possibly any premiums).

3. Premiums, Deductibles, and Copays: First Budget for them

Establish a Budget to Prepare for Medical Costs. When you think of being prepared, what types of emergencies come to mind? Remember that the specific premiums and out-of-pocket costs will vary based on your plan, so review your Medicare and supplemental insurance policies for a reasonable estimate.

4. Future Healthcare Needs

Healthcare needs usually increase as we age, and planning for these future costs is more complicated. If you answered that almost everything was fine and normal, perhaps it is too easy to dismiss your future self. That said, budgeting conservatively (and planning for a more significant future medical expenditure) will prepare you for higher healthcare expenses.

Factoring Inflation: Since healthcare costs generally increase more than the standard inflation rate, account for that when projecting future expenditures. It is a safe bet that healthcare expenses will rise 5-7% per year over time.

5. Look into Spousal Health Insurance

But if your spouse is not qualified for Medicare or has different healthcare needs, make sure to budget in payments for their healthcare, too. That could mean buying an individual policy until they qualify for Medicare. This can save financial burden and allow both to be well covered, subsequently planning for the healthcare needs of each partner.

Balancing the Present & Future of Healthcare Costs

Knowing what the healthcare plan is allows for long-term cost management. Here are some financial tricks to help you stay afloat while getting necessary healthcare.

- Review Your Plan Annually

Reviewing your Medicare or Medicare Advantage plans yearly is essential because they can change yearly. You can adjust your plan during Open Enrollment (Oct 15-Dec 7) if needed. Income changes may impact premiums, deductibles, or benefits that you should carefully review to make sure these elements of your coverage continue to meet your needs.

- Utilize Preventive Services

At no cost, Medicare provides various preventive services, including screenings, vaccinations, and wellness visits. The use of these services can help catch potential health issues early on, aiming to reduce expensive treatments in the future. Proactive health care is one of the most effective strategies for containing medical costs in retirement.

- Look into Assistance Programs

Many programs provide additional help with health care costs for people who have low incomes and assets, including retirees. Medicaid, Medicare

CHAPTER 7

Tax-Sensitive Withdrawals Strategies

After all, when you think of retirement planning, taxes are not usually the first thing that comes to mind. Yet, reducing taxes on your withdrawals could help explain the difference between outliving your savings or not and having a pleasant retirement instead of constantly worrying about running out of money. The less you pay in taxes, the more money can stay where it belongs... It is in your pocket so you can realize someday that getting older will be somewhat enjoyable (instead of a total financial worry). Tax efficiency is not an added perk in retirement planning; it's a basic strategy. In this chapter, I'd like to show you how a few tax-sensitive withdrawal strategies can help your retirement account withdrawals last longer. I'll also introduce the concept of Roth IRAs and demonstrate ways to minimize taxes on potential time bombs in your Deferred accounts, allowing you to withdraw more money.

Taxable, Tax-Deferred and Tax-Free Accounts

Getting more specific into tactics later, we begin with a brief overview of your account types and how they are taxed. Different types of accounts come with different tax implications and benefits, so it is essential to know these differences.

1. Taxable Accounts

Taxable accounts, like brokerage accounts, are funded with post-tax dollars. Contributions are not tax-deductible, but you save on the only time that all your earnings (lobby or gains) and dividends will be taxed when an investment is sold out/earning interest.

Capital Gains Tax: When you sell an investment for more than its initial cost price in a taxable account, that profit is subject to capital gains tax. The taxes you'll pay depend on how long you own the investment: short-term gains (those collected in less than a year) are taxed at ordinary income rates, while long-term gains (ones set up for more than a year) qualify for lower capital gains tax.

Dividends and Interest: Dividend or interest income is generally taxable in the year earned, except that qualified dividends may be eligible for decreased tax rates.

2. Tax-Deferred Accounts

Tax-Deferred Accounts: If you save in tax-deferred accounts, such as traditional IRAs and 401(k)s — which include pre-tax contributions to the account (earnings are also never taxed) but withdrawals that are taxed at ordinary income rates upon distribution. The upside here is that your savings grow without taxes until you withdraw the gains, which allows for more significant growth over time.

Taxation of Withdrawals: The portions of your withdrawals representing amounts initially contributed to a tax-deferred account are taxable at ordinary income rates, no matter how long you have held the investments. This is particularly relevant for retirees since it would mean that any dollar they take from a traditional IRA or 401(k) in retirement, even if used to pay income taxes, will increase their taxable income at the time of withdrawal.

Required MINIMUM Distribution (RMD): Starting at age 73 ~ in 2024, the IRS starts REQUIRING that you take $$$ from your pre-tax accounts, Period. Not taking these withdrawals can lead to significant fines, regardless of whether you want the funds.

3. Tax-Free Accounts

Since Roth IRAs and Roth 401(k)s are accounts that do not tax the money as you withdraw it, this is a unique advantage for people who retire. You save after-tax dollars for these accounts, but qualified withdrawals in retirement are free from taxes. Combined with a tax-deferred account, winning and losing can be the difference.

Roth IRAs have no RMDs. With traditional IRAs, you must take a minimum distribution amount each year starting at age 70½; Roth IRA funds can continue growing tax-free indefinitely.

Qualified withdrawals — if you are over 59½ and the Roth account has been open for at least five years, a tax-free way to increase your retirement income.

How to Optimize Tax Reduction on the Withdrawal Process

Now that we understand the three retirement account types, let's see how you can liquidate them to maximize after-tax wealth. The order you pull from all your accounts can differ each year, and its impact on your tax liability will also vary, so creating a withdrawal strategy cannot be taken lightly.

1. Start with Taxable Accounts First

Instead, it may be more appropriate to tap into taxable investment accounts. The long-term capital gains tax rate is usually lower than the ordinary income tax rate, so selling appreciated investments can offer you a significant advantage. This will also let your pre-tax and after-tax accounts continue to compound.

Thus, if you have a taxable account with stocks, bonds, and other assets in it even now using "Location" principles (Putting the most tax-inefficient funds into your retirement investment accounts) — sell appreciated non-public business interests/real estate or anything similarly tax-wise friendly that has been held for at least one year.

Moreover, this plan helps lower tax brackets (at least in the early retirement years).

2. Utilize Required Minimum Distributions and Tax-Deferred Accounts

At age 73, you must take RMDs from your pre-tax accounts. As ordinary income, planning the withdrawals you take from your 401(k) or traditional IRA is necessary to prevent large tax spikes. You should withdraw the least amount necessary (since they will be siblings in your taxable income).

Another approach that can make sense is to take partial withdrawals from tax-deferred accounts in the years before hitting the milestone age of 73. This can help you smooth out the tax hit over time instead of hitting a vast, lump-sum tax bill during RMDs.

3. ROTH Accounts for Tax-Free Withdrawals

Qualified withdrawals from a Roth IRA are more accessible to make in retirement and entirely tax-free. If you have both Roth and traditional IRAs, consider taking a few dollars out of the Roths to make your withdrawals more tax-efficient. For example, if you're destined to be in a higher tax bracket because of other income —and taxes paid on Social Security might help make that happen—taking money from a Roth IRA instead of or through your traditional IRA could keep you out of the danger zone.

This can also be beneficial in the case of an unexpected expense; it has the added capability to allow you to withdraw money without growing your tax bill. This adaptability is valuable regarding tax efficiency because it enables you to efficiently target your taxable income level.

4. Roth Conversion Strategy

On the other hand, a Roth conversion refers to moving money from a traditional IRA or 401(k) into any account under the Roth umbrella. However, you will be taxed on the converted amount immediately following that, and any withdrawals in retirement from your Roth IRA are tax-free. When done correctly, this is a potent strategy in retirement.

Timing: This is ideal for Roth conversion during low-income years (the period between retirement and RMD initiation). In these years, you might be in a lower tax bracket, so converting funds from your traditional IRA into a Roth may make sense.

Splitting—Converting smaller amounts over several years is likely less tax-efficient than converting the total amount in one year. This extends the tax effect and allows you to utilize cheaper tax brackets.

5. Claim as Many Tax Credits/Deductions as Possible —

Use tax credits and deductions – they can reduce the taxable income you must claim in retirement. For example, charitable contributions help us feel good and may result in lower taxes. For those of you who are 70½ or older, a Qualified Charitable Distribution (QCD) from your IRA is eligible for an up-to-$100-thousand donation annually, tax-free. QCDs count toward your RMD, but as I just mentioned, since you are killing two birds with one stone, 100% of the distribution is effectively coming out tax-free, reducing taxable income.

Bunching deductions:

The standard deduction will be more significant if you combine deductible expenses for two years into one year. This could be useful to lower your taxable income in specific years (e.g. if you have high medical expenses or charitable contributions).

Using Roth IRAs and Tax-Deferred Accounts in Retirement

Considering the previous points, Roth IRAs and tax-deferred accounts should be used together in a well-balanced retirement plan to maximize efficiency. So, how do you make the most of them this way?

1. Begin with Tax-Deferred and Transition to Roth

One common strategy is to front-load the drawdown of tax-deferred accounts while in retirement before RMDs kick in. That way, your Roth account can continue to grow tax-free. When you have to start taking RMDs, your balance in tax-deferred accounts will likely already be reduced, so the required distributions are smaller and more manageable on year-end taxes.

Roth funds can also help shield you from inflation if utilized later in retirement, as withdrawals are tax-free and do not push your taxable income into the next bracket.

2. Legacy Strategy Roth Funds

If you want part of your plan to include leaving a financial legacy, Roth IRAs can be powerful tools for heirs. In contrast to tax-deferred accounts, Roth IRAs are inherited income tax-free, so your beneficiaries can draw from the funds without being required to pay any upfront taxes.

More Tax-Efficient Strategies

But there are also a few other ways to limit the taxes you pay in retirement.

1. Understand State Tax Considerations

TY: You have to live someplace else in retirement based on taxes. So you have to look at which states don't tax income in one of the stable previous lessons and how much they levy on retirement earnings for those who do. When planning to retire in a low- or even no-tax state, look up the tax cow to best understand which states may be on your radar...and those you want to nest at all.

2. Use Health Savings Accounts (HSAs)

If you qualify, look into funding a Health Savings Account (HSA), which allows tax-free savings for qualified medical expenses. In retirement, you can still use tax-free withdrawals from an HSA to pay for healthcare expenses that reduce your taxable income.

3. Diversify Your Income Sources

All three types of accounts lead to flexibility and tax control each year. This diversification allows you to pull on different account types based on your tax situation to control the taxation of your retirement income.

CHAPTER 8

Making the Right Retirement Housing Decisions

Housing decisions can be one of many retirees' more crucial (and sometimes complicated) components of retirement planning. Yes, your house may have worked for you during those years in the workforce, but now you need to reevaluate whether it still works and fits into today's lifestyle. The decision of whether to downsize or relocate is a common one for those entering retirement, but it involves more than simply choosing where you want your next home. The Things to Consider When Looking for a Retirement Home: From Downsizing, Relocating and How You Can Release Equity from Your Existing Home to remodel Your Life. By getting to know what lifestyles there are, you can more easily sort out which one fits your financial goals and personal needs for the time being.

Is Downsizing an Option?

- Downsizing

To have additional cash, simplify your life, and reduce the workload of home management. Many retirees don't need all the space they have while raising a family or working full-time. Sure, downsizing means you can fit your life into a little more than a matchbox when the time is right to retire.

1. The Money Aspect of Downsizing

Downsizing – The financial benefits of downsizing can be quick and significant. If you live in a larger or more expensive home, selling your current house and downsizing to something smaller could help unlock... You can then reinvest this equity to generate retirement income, pay off debts, or spend it traveling the world and pursuing hobbies you have been waiting for years. Downsizing also cuts costs in property taxes, homeowners' insurance, and even essential utilities or maintenance.

When, for instance, a retiree sells his $500,000 family home and buys a condo at 60% of that price tag, he can park another

$200K in cash from the deal, too, e.g., invest, spend, fulfill other priorities, etc..... This also means that the monthly cost of living could be much more consistent and controllable as property taxes are lower.

2. Downsizing Your Lifestyle

Not only does downsizing come with financial rewards, it typically imparts a simplified way of living. A larger home is more demanding on your body and bank account as the years go by, so moving to a smaller place takes the pressure off. Condos, townhouses, or retirement communities with homeowners' associations (HOA) that provide lawn care and snow removal services are popular among retirees. That means more time for family fun, hobbies, and travel.

3. Considerations Before Downsizing

While they may offer a more seductive proposition than cramming America into oblivion, here are some reasons to be suspicious of the downsizing label:

- Location

Can the person receive healthcare, see their family, and enjoy social activities in a new place? Being close to these things is vital.

- Home Equity + Market Conditions:

Timing: It may be a brilliant idea to sell if housing prices in your area are high simply. On the other hand, if you wait until a seller's market, your home could be worth much more.

Con: Cost The most significant negative of moving is that it can be incredibly pricey, between realtor fees and the cost to move and perhaps renovate. Just ensure these costs do not exceed the financial benefits of moving to a smaller home.

For others, it offers a meaningful retirement lifestyle option to align with your financial planning and goals.

- Moving: Select a New Hometown

Retirement is your chance to lead a completely new life, which can mean wanting to move somewhere sunnier or possibly cheaper. Retirees looking to escape harsh winters or just reduce expenses and be closer to the family have plenty of options whether they prefer active urban environments like San Diego or Miami, where the median home price is $2.7 million for pre-retirees versus affordable, comfortable neighborhoods in places like Muncie well within their retirement income budget of $63 spent on a house over time considering renovation costs with a wide range from 1% up the cost per hours savings incurred from lowest end fixer upper conversions back down here at impresoscope level ROC.

How Relocating Affects Your Finances

It can also result in direct cost savings—for example, if you move to a less expensive location or into an area with lower property taxes. Vermont and Colorado are Examples. Vermont has various tax benefits for retirees, including no estate or sales taxes (one state we chose due to exemptions). One advantage of relocating to a tax-friendly state in retirement is that it gives you more money, too.

Of course, there are also costs associated with moving. Often, the move is not local to where the family lives, so you must visit home, which means that plane fare and other expenses (furniture) would be involved. You must calculate these costs and compare them with possible savings to affirm if moving would benefit your budget.

2. Evaluating Lifestyle Changes

Lifestyle is an essential consideration in any decision to move. Think about home life in the new location.

- Weather

Do you like being a little warmer all year round or enjoy having four seasons? Consider how the surroundings influence your health, comfort, and pastimes.

- Community

Retirement is about social connections, so evaluate how easy it will be to make new friends there. Research social events, clubs, and amenities for seniors in the new area.

- Health Care Accessibility

As we age, our health and proximity to good healthcare must become easily accessible. The area should have decent healthcare, especially for our unique medical needs.

Careful consideration of these time, budget, and convenience components can result in a rewarding destination for your retirement.

Equity Release: A Way to Unlock Your Home's Value

If you do not wish to sell or move home, you can still unlock the value of your property via equity release. There are several ways to do this, each with pros and cons.

1. Home Equity Loans and Home Equity Lines of Credit

A home equity loan or a HELOC (home equity line of credit) allows you to borrow against the value of your house while still owning it. This can be perfect for a retiree who may not require access to credit but wants to maintain their home.

Home equity loan — lump sum, reasonable for one-time expenses or projects (e.g., home renovations/medical bills). A specific part of the loan must be repaid over time as principal and interest, but fees are typically lower than other types.

HELOC: A HELOC allows you to borrow what you want when... The repayment type for a HELOC is usually interest-only during the draw period, and the total payback will occur later.

Although these loans are cheap, they place a lien on your house, so you need to make sure the numbers work and have an exit strategy if things go wrong instead of facing foreclosure.

2. Reverse Mortgage

A reverse mortgage is a loan that homeowners 62 years or older can take out in cash straight from their home equity. Repayment comes only when the homeowner sells his residence or dies. Retirees like reverse mortgages because they have no monthly payments and can stay in their homes.

Pros: The income is tax-free, and there are no monthly payments. The family keeps the home, regardless of how much is borrowed, and your heirs can pay off the loan to own or sell the house.

Cons: The fees and interest rates on reverse mortgages may be higher than those on other loans. They also reduce the equity in your home. You are also responsible for maintaining the house and paying property taxes and insurance.

A reverse mortgage might be a sensible solution if you plan on keeping your house long-term and think it makes sense to earn an income slowly while eliminating monthly payments.

Understanding Home Modifications in Preparation for Retirement

If aging in place is your goal, home modifications can create a safer and more accessible environment. If you are planning to retire, more and more people are choosing semi-retirement or retirement at home when living in a new house is too expensive.

1. Typical Safety and Accessibility Changes

Repurposing the bathroom: Adding grab bars, installing a walk-in shower, and setting up an elevated toilet can make bathrooms less hazardous for occupants of all ages.

Stair Answers: Installing stairlifts or developmental ramps can further assist people with disabilities in those multi-story homes. Others will remodel the first floor off of a family room or den into a bedroom (or) instead.

Improved lighting: Better lighting and better light fittings can reduce the risk of falls and make moving around your home at night easier. Non-slip flooring

2. Budgeting for Modifications

They can be as small as a few modifications or more significant-scale remodeling. Costs can span expenses, so establishing a budget and making alterations at the top of one's mind is essential regarding needs/safety. An assortment of upgrades, such as grab bars for your bathroom or floor plan changes like installing a stairlift, can range from low-cost to a few thousand dollars. Be sure to cover all costs and check if any grants or senior funding is available.

3. Funding Options

Modifying your home can be funded through personal savings, a home equity loan, or the VA Assistance Program. There are some organizations and state programs where you may qualify for grants or low-interest loans to help pay for home modifications when seeking at-home senior care.

CHAPTER 9

How to Protect Your Assets in Retirement

Looking after your money should be about wise financial management and putting a security plan around to pave the way for your legacy and the direction of what you worked so hard to accumulate. In these situations, estate planning and legal protections are needed. Asset protection is more than just planning; it also wouldn't be complete if you do not use the right tools, utilize tested strategies, and properly manage those assets to ensure they are well protected from risks. We will discuss the basics of asset protection in retirement, what legal protections are necessary as you enter your golden years, and explore estate planning documents anyone over 50 needs to have on hand. Ultimately, you will understand how to build a secure and resilient plan for your assets.

1. Building Respect for Asset Protection – The Rules

The root concept of asset protection is to secure the wealth you have built from broader, cloaked, unanticipated risks, unfounded legal claims, or inescapable taxation. The following are a few key areas to consider when implementing legal measures that protect your assets:

Wills and Living Trusts

For most people, an estate plan starts with a will or living trust, defining how their assets will be distributed and who is to inherit from them. If you pass away without a will, your assets could be put through probate (which is not only time-dependent but also public), and the distribution of those tangible items might not reflect what you would have preferred.

Wills—A will determine who gets your stuff when you pass away and allows you to appoint beneficiaries of various assets and an executor in charge of handling administration. Will must go through probate, meaning your heirs can be tied up in red tape and legal fees.

Avoiding Probate: Living Trusts Instead of a will, living trusts can avoid probate and make it easier to transfer assets. While you are living, though unable to after your passing, the same is true of a revocable trust where life keeps on, and part of that could be directing who will succeed as trustee. It can allow for more privacy and might lessen some of the costs related to an estate.

Durable Power of Attorney

A power of attorney (POA) is one of the most important documents. This document allows you to designate someone with authority over your financial or legal matters when you can no longer make these decisions. This can include power over your wallet, paying bills, handling property, and other economic issues. A strong POA can help avoid guardianship, which requires family members to proceed through the court system and is often expensive and time-consuming.

Medical Power of Attorney and Living Will

A healthcare power of attorney (also called a medical POA) is when you choose someone to handle your care decisions if you cannot. Usually, this will be combined with an advance directive or living will that details what treatments and procedures you want (or do not want) to receive at the end of your life. Then came the stressing over his private directives. These documents help ensure medical requests are revered and keep your loved ones from fighting alone about what you might have needed (or no longer wanted) in a favorable clinical situation.

Beneficiary Designations

Most people focus on wills and trusts, but beneficiary designations are just as important. Some financial accounts — like retirement or life insurance policies and others- permit you to name beneficiaries, which indicates that these assets can be transferred outside of probate. It would be best to keep your designations current to ensure that a document reflects what you want, especially after life events like marriage or divorce and children's birth.

TOD & POD (Transfer on Death/Payable upon Death) Accounts

You can include a TOD designation for investment accounts and wrangle with beneficiaries without going through probate, whereas bank account POD designations are already fairly common. These designations function similarly to beneficiary designations on retirement accounts, which would then flow directly to your heirs without being probated. These are the most effective methods to transfer assets quickly and easily.

2. Wealth Protection: Key Tips to Reduce Risks

After addressing legal safeguards, you can consider the risks that could destroy your wealth. Every facet of your financial life can be somewhat shielded, and many have several strategies available anytime.

Umbrella Insurance

Umbrella insurance gives you extra liability protection on top of what your home and auto policies already cover. You are shielded from humongous claims or lawsuits, and you can avoid covering such liability risks as a car accident, someone getting hurt on your property, or accidentally damaging another person's things. These relatively low-cost policies might give you peace of mind in knowing your assets, on top of balances over car insurance for teens and adults, with a few tips to get cheap teen auto insurance, especially when employment benefits such as umbrella coverage sound like.

Long-Term Care Insurance

Long-term care: One of the most significant threats to retirement assets is long-term care. One important distinction to make is that long-term care expenses are not covered under Medicare, meaning if you live a long life and need significant help in your later years (like some 70%+ of Americans over age 65 do), all the savings discussed above can be eaten up by those costs. Long-Term Care Insurance = insurance that helps pay for in-home care, assisted living, or a nursing home. Purchasing this insurance in your late 50s or early 60s may also give you more broad coverage at a lower premium than many other types of caregiving services, which can protect your retirement savings from significantly impacting health care costs.

Asset Protection Trusts

Asset protection trusts are a mechanism built to protect your assets from creditors, lawsuits, or any other risk you might face in terms of financial loss. This can be a domestic or offshore trust, and the asset protection level varies depending on state and international laws. An asset protection trust can work well for someone who wants to guarantee a "buffer" of their wealth is shielded from lawsuits, such as many retirees. Qualifying Domestic Asset Protection, Trust These should be created long before there are any claims or lawsuits in favor of a creditor—and for sure not as partaking with a view to litigation.

Gifts & Charitable Giving

An estate plan can lower tax bills by providing for gifting of unique assets during your life. According to the IRS, when it comes to gifting, no one gets punished during their lifetime for doing so because once money has been taxed in your name as income, you are free and clear if ever giving any part of what is left over (whether cash or property) away.

Under the annual gift tax exclusion offered by the Internal Revenue Service1), an individual may receive gifts totaling up to $17.00 for each recipient/recipient (or deadweight burden on right nomocracy issuing before taxable state has reached limits imposed under actuator rights mandatory thermograve assessment which come from excluded absolute trust face provision-based database document contributor fulcrum simple bilateral identification process ascertain week Presently 2024).

Further, charitable donations provide an opportunity for estate concern with immediate tax deductions and reduction of the taxable amount, which means you can help the causes supporting you in the event of your death alongside cutting off some parts on taxes.

Charitable Remainder Trust (CRT) – A CRT allows you to give assets in a trust and receive the income generated by those assets during your lifetime. Then, the principal will go to charity. This gives you an income stream while reducing your estate's overall value.

3. Estate Planning & Tax Minimization

You want your assets to go to the person or institution you intended, but also seek out individuals who can minimize what will happen in a preference manner down upon your heirs. With appropriate tax minimization strategies, you can ensure that even more money remains behind for your non-charitable beneficiaries.

Roth IRA Conversions

Convert some of the funds in your traditional IRAs to a Roth IRA if you have them. You are charged taxes on the dollar amount that was converted in a given year when converting to Roth, however for every other subsequent fulfilling tax year at least) It enjoys all unabated growth during retirement and does not require RMDs (minimum distributions required). If you anticipate that your heirs will fall into a higher tax bracket, consider going this route so they can receive Roth distributions free from income taxes.

Grantor Retained Annuity Trust (GRAT).

A GRAT is a powerful estate planning tool that enables you to transfer assets into a trust for family members (or others) with limited gift tax implications. A GRAT is a trust where you place assets in the trust and get back an annuity payment for a specified number of years. At the end of the term, whatever value is left to your beneficiaries passes free from estate and gift taxes. This tactic is especially effective with assets you believe will appreciate dramatically, as it enables you to capture current value and pass along any appreciation in the asset tax-free to your beneficiaries.

A Family Limited Partnership (FLP) is one of the most popular forms.

Family Limited Partnerships (LP): An LP is a business entity that you can use to transfer assets to family members while still keeping control of those assets (s). Gifting FLP shares to relatives can also decrease the taxable value of your estate (discounts are generally applied when apprising gifted shares). FLPs are intricate mechanisms that must be managed with extreme care to satisfy the step transaction doctrine. However, when utilized appropriately by high-net-worth families, they can offer significant estate tax savings.

Qualified Personal Residence Trust (QPRT) Restricts the transfer of a residence again; an irrevocable trust allows you to gift your interests in real estate without attendant appreciation, generally escaping outright because it utilizes up some or all of the estate tax credit.

A QPRT is an irrevocable trust that may make sense if you have a high-value home and would like to give it away while retaining the right to live in your house for several years. After this period, the house is lowered into beneficiaries at a reduced tax value, lowering total estate taxes. AQPRTs are helpful for individuals who desire to transfer their family homestead while minimizing taxes.

CHAPTER 10

How to Live Healthy in Retirement (Physically, Emotionally and Mentally)

Divorce is said to be a new beginning so that in retirement, you can rediscover yourself, what interests you, and, most importantly, your health welfare. Physical, emotional, and mental well-being must remain intact so that these years can be enjoyed. Living right is the key to a longer life and ensures you have all the energy and vigor to indulge in everything that brings happiness. In this chapter, I will help you discover approaches to ensure that acting remains a component of your identity and keeps both of your well-being in retirement. When you resign, it will cover how to make exercise a part of your lifestyle and mental health practices to ensure a happy mind.

In this thrilling phase of life, you have an excellent opportunity to work towards fulfillment and joy.

How to Live A Healthy, Physically Active Life

Physical activity is one of the best ways to stay healthy and maintain retirement independence. Regular movement can help keep your muscles firm, increase flexibility, and maintain a healthy cardiovascular system, ensuring you are more mobile for longer and reducing the risk of fall injuries.

1. Creating a Physical Activity Routine

Your workouts do not have to be in the gym or long and grueling. The trick with exercise is to start doing things you enjoy, and then it will happen regularly. Aerobic exercise (walking, bicycling, swimming, and dancing) helps keep the heart healthy while gently allowing one to enjoy daily movement. The CDC suggests at least 150 minutes of moderate-intensity aerobic activity.

This physical activity can keep the muscles strong as we age. Weightlifting (or resistance bands or bodyweight exercises like squats and push-ups) can be a powerful ally in the fight against muscle loss.

TODO: Strength training a minimum of two days per week.

The Flexibility-And-Balance:

Exercising like yoga or tai chi will help you be more mobile and lessen your chances of falling. These exercises significantly help with posture and range of motion, making everyday tasks more accessible to your body. If you are new to fitness or have longstanding health conditions, you might want to find a trainer specializing in training seniors. They can help you create a safe and effective program based on your capabilities.

2. We live in a sedentary world.

If you find that prioritizing a workout is challenging, start including movement in your day: Your Feet are the New Tires—walk whenever possible. Take a walk after meals or park farther away from your destination. That is good for your digestion and circulation. Even the little walks are much better than nothing.

- Stretch while watching TV

Stand up and stretch or take a few quick exercises during commercial breaks.

- Physical Activity at Home:

Gardening, cleaning, or throwing a dance party in your living room are simple ways to get off the couch and keep moving.

Doing small things to add up the amount of activity you do throughout your day can eventually have significant health impacts on people. As always — any movement is good.

3. A Sound Nutrition Plan for Good Health.

Get energized by fueling your body with proper nutrition, not just exercise. A healthy diet helps support your activities, maintain weight, and provide the nutrients you need for good health.

- The Goal

Eat good food. Whole foods, including fruits, vegetables, and whole grains; lean proteins such as fish; milk... In most cases, your diet is crucial in preparing carefully prepared branded foods that contain primarily natural products from fruit and veggies that you need to eat anyway.

- Hydrate Regularly:

The older we get, the more our thirst perception decreases; hence, it is easier to hydrate deficient from dehydration. Shoot for around eight cups — but adjust as necessary based on your activity level and the climate in which you live.

- Avoid Processed Foods

These foods contain excess sodium, trans fats, and added sugars. Eating less of these can do wonders for your heart and weight.

If you are already following a nutrition plan, great, but if you are dealing with health-specific issues or conditions (including diabetics and high blood pressure), maybe consult a Nutritionist to get your meal plans personalized according to the goals for which they were created.

Caring for the Mind and Emotions

In retirement, as in life generally, formal physical health is complemented by an equal need for self-regulation of emotional and mental well-being. For those who are retired, it can be tempting to call work a respite because as much relief comes from leaving the answerability of job life, so is there also with its departure an emptiness in time and outed (is that even a word) for one must use or lose their good mental health.

1. Staying Socially Connected

Strong social connections are crucial for improving our moods and quality of life. It helps to prevent isolation, which is essential for preventing depression and possible cognitive decline as well.

- Create a Social Routine

If you have regular dates with family, friends, or neighbors. Maybe you plan weekly coffee dates, join social clubs, or volunteer in your town. This way, you can keep on track and even look forward to a week of socializing.

Join New Clubs

Want to read more, do some gardening, or explore a new creative outlet? These clubs can help you stay in tune with life, feel like a living being, and be social about something that interests you.

- Stay in Touch Virtually

If you are a few miles away from your loved ones and they can't come over for facial expressions, " pick up the phone. You can stay in touch with loved ones and meet new friends via video calls, social media, or online groups.

A strong social network can boost emotional resilience and increase well-being throughout retirement.

2. Brain work & lifelong learning

- The MSGMayer column by Another take

use it or lose it. My mom has been driving me crazy lately about keeping my brain active and minimizing the effects of aging on her mental faculties. The good news is that there are endless ways to keep the brain moving and you entertained. Do Something Satisfying That Challenges Your Brain Activities such as puzzles, reading, or playing musical instruments are a lot of fun and good for mental health. You can also pick up a new hobby, such as learning to paint or photograph, or even learn another language.

- Continue Taking Classes

Many classes are available for seniors at local universities, community centers, and libraries. A class, whether in history, literature, or technology, warms the noggin and keeps freelancer engagement up to par.

- Partake in Memory Exercises

Games such as Sudoku, chess, or other specific exercises can also improve cognitive function. There are several apps and websites out there to help you stay sane with games that keep your brain in good shape.

3. Managing Stress and Building Resilience Full-Length Transcription

Even in retirement, you are not immune to stress, and we must manage our day-to-day lives with the proper perspective. The good news is that countless methods exist to develop and hone those abilities.

- Use Mindfulness and Meditation

Mindfulness strategies can also improve emotion regulation, reduce stress, and lower blood pressure. Just 5-10 minutes of meditation daily can make an incredible difference in mood and mental clarity.

- Establish Personal Objectives

Once goals have been created, determine what will give your life a sense of meaning and direction. So you know, things like — finishing a book, walking for X km or visiting Y place. Measuring what you are doing can help your feeling of accomplishment and motivation.

- Practice gratitude

Take time to reflect and express appreciation for what you are grateful for, which can increase your positive emotions. Begin writing in a gratitude journal, where you write three things each day that make you happy. You are designed, even though it might not feel like that sometimes, TO be able to handle whatever ups and downs life gives you.

The Issue with a Retirement Health Plan

To do it well, health and wellness in retirement must become part of the fabric of a happy life that includes physical, mental, and emotional practices woven into a balanced routine. Of course, if you feel good, the rest of your life seems to fall into place. Here is how to attain a more holistic health plan to keep feeling amazing and performing at optimum levels!

1. Set Personal Health Goals

Begin setting attainable health goals that are aligned with your values. These may include exercise goals (walking 30 minutes daily), mental health goals, or learning new skills. Establish deadlines for every goal and monitor your progress; congratulate yourself on the little things.

2. Schedule Regular Check-Ins

Getting some standard health checks done will play a crucial role in detecting an illness. Make regular appointments with your healthcare providers for screenings, vaccinations, and other preventive practices. Maintain Health Precautions – By monitoring your health, you can prevent minor issues from getting more significant.

3. Prioritize Sleep and Rest

The foundation of all things physical and mental health is a good nap. Try to get 7-8 hours of good quality sleep. Implementing a relaxing bedtime routine, minimizing screen time before bed, and cultivating an ideal sleep environment can significantly enhance your snooze.

4. Balance Rest with Activity

Exercising is necessary, but it is equally important as giving your body rest. Take rest days, and get active on others by doing mild exercises such as stretching and yoga to prevent your body from getting out of kilter.

5. Create a Support System

A social network is a source of well-being and health in itself. Share your goals with family and friends to hold you accountable; better yet, they can participate in yearly activities. If you want to be responsible, hire a coach or join a group who will ensure that they do not let up on your dedication to entering minimal viable healthiness.

CHAPTER 11

Achieving Financial Freedom in Retirement

Financial freedom in retirement is not just about having enough money to last you the rest of your life; it also means being secure and self-sufficient so that if others need or want help, you can offer assistance without sacrificing comfort. This freedom, however, is a double-edged sword because this kind of solo travel also brings some responsibilities to yourself and the people around you. Juggling independence and honest financial management could be a blessing in disguise to prevent common mistakes from overspending, running, and begging for more money from Mother, Dad, or Uncle Tommy. What will they do to maintain their financial independence? How can they effectively balance freedom with responsibility and avoid relying on family members for money?

You can create a secure and meaningful retirement through thoughtful preparation — uniquely your own.

Understanding Financial Freedom During Retirement

For example, being financially free in retirement implies that you are adequately funded to manage your basic lifestyle expenses, prepare for any unexpected or discretionary items, and have the money to come up with the necessary cash when an emergency presents itself. Those may include an income plan providing essential living needs, health costs, vacations, or something personal to the saver. It is about having options—whether that means traveling, picking up hobbies, or just living without worrying about where the money will come from.

It is not simply about creating alpha (wealth) — only with beta can we achieve true financial freedom. Establishing a reliable method of generating income for long-term investments, pensions, or social security savings will allow you to live confidently and avoid asking other people.

Freedom and Responsibility are not opposite poles...but the best of friends...

Financial freedom means you can kick back, but now it's time to manage resources wisely for retirement longevity. Here are some of the best ways to maintain this balance actively:

1. Setting a Realistic Budget

Budgeting is just a practical device that enables you to trace spending, determine requirements, and set your goals for future years. So, although it may feel like a straitjacket, budgeting will allow you to make informed decisions on how and when to spend your money. You release categories through which you can illustrate if your expenses are centered on housing, food, transport repairs, health, or entertainment.

Fit the necessities (especially healthcare and housing) into your budget and keep them as close as possible to a well-oiled machine that doesn't grind all other categories to a halt. This will enable you to be free and, at the same time, operate under control so you can feel a taste of life without killing all fundamentals.

2. Managing Debt Wisely

As someone who retired with lots of debt, Camino saw how carrying that financial burden could compromise retirement in a way where you might be able to cover basic needs only — and might have an easier time convincing relatives to open their wallets. Try to pay off, or at least down, high-interest debt like credit card balances before you retire if feasible. For starters, in retirement, work on preventing new debt from appearing.

Balance your monthly debt and loan payments like mortgage or car payments with the income you will have in retirement to be sure that those obligations do not burden your lifestyle. Taking care of your debt responsibly gives you the freedom that financial flexibility can bring, which means no overdue liabilities.

3. Diversifying Income Streams

With a diversified portfolio of income streams, you have more than one source of revenue, which means that if something happens to the one you're currently using, it is not detrimental. Mix Social Security with retirement accounts, dividend income from investments, rent checks, or even part-time work to diversify your sources of money so that if market conditions or other economic factors whack one, the others pick up some slack.

It involves considering multiple buckets of money to balance income vs. tax efficiency. For instance, it is also wise to start by pulling from taxable accounts and then let your tax-advantaged accumulation grow.

4. Planning for Healthcare Costs

Healthcare is typically one of the most significant expenses in retirement, and knowing how much you can expect to pay for planned healthcare needs and surprises will make a huge difference. You may need to purchase supplemental or long-term care insurance in addition to Medicare. HSA balances can only be used for healthcare expenses, which minimizes the risk of high medical costs, eating away at your more considerable retirement savings.

If you have a Health Savings Account (HSA), which is also a great savings tool for paying for medical expenses through tax-free withdrawals, an emergency fund for health costs provides a financial safety net of sorts, and there is all the more reason to have one even if an HSA isn't on your plate.

5. Taking the Long View: Your Estate Plan And Legacy

When planning our finances for retirement, we must think today about what we want to leave when the end of time catches up. A will, trusts if necessary, and beneficiaries for your accounts are steps toward a defined legacy plan. It is not strictly a matter of bequeathing wealth; it also involves identifying what decisions will express your values, safeguard your family, and advance the causes you believe in.

The establishment that people aged 18 and up everywhere say no to, the dying one: estate planning so taxes are minimized and your assets go where you decide—not the government. In its stride, this reduces the risk of financial dependency as a family would not be faced with making decisions on your behalf that you may or may never have wanted, and clarity is also rooted in [needless] access to your account.

How to Stay Financially Independent and not depend on your Family

One of the most challenging things about retirement is ensuring you do not become a fiscal liability to your family. Receiving mortgage help for children or budget assistance with their own families to care for, most retirees do not wish to burden relatives by adding financial stress.

Here are a few practical ways to not rely on your family and, at the same time, stay financially independent.

1. Create an Emergency Fund

An emergency fund is a way to financially protect yourself from unexpected expenses = not going back home. The purpose of having an emergency fund is to cover three to six months of essential expenses such as health, housing, and extra costs. When you hold onto this fund as a standalone account and do not mix it with your retirement savings, you can redeem the amounts quickly if necessary.

An emergency fund guards your finances and relationships by allowing you to deal with unexpected expenses without worrying loved ones or taking on additional debt.

2. Choose your Housing Wisely

Since housing is typically the single most significant retirement expenditure, it's essential to choose wisely, regardless of your financial situation. Moving to a cheaper location or paying off your mortgage are ways of reducing monthly bills and lifting the weight of personal finances.

3. Review your Insurance Coverage Regularly

Adequate insurance coverage is essential for your financial independence. You can cover areas besides health insurance, such as a long-term care policy, umbrella liability insurance, or home insurance. All of these coverages have their essential role in keeping your assets covered and assisting you with various bills that could come up.

Keeping your insurance up-to-date means the policy fits your needs at a given time and decreases the chances that others will have to pay costs out of pocket.

4. Leave Within Your Means

Living below your lifestyle doesn't mean you cannot have fun; it means living within the limits of what is possible over an extended period. Do not buy a sports car or take expensive vacations, which would deplete your retirement savings. Lastly, remember that financial independence often entails changing one's perspective from consumptive to experience-based living centered on relationships, hobbies, and self-fulfillment.

Adhering to a reasonable budget helps you maintain financial stability and ensures that your money is available for necessities so that you do not have to rely on outside help.

5. Conversation with Family regarding Finances

Knowing your numbers and discussing them openly with your family can avoid misunderstandings and create a healthy environment. Communicate your financial goals, budget, and plans for healthcare or long-term care so loved ones are aware of their future obligations. They will appreciate that you both have taken steps to stay self-reliant, and these discussions will build trust.

When someone offers to help you pay for school, do some prayerful introspection before accepting or declining their assistance. Although the help of a family member may be helpful in some instances, it is essential to ensure that the support does not accidentally facilitate dependency or create tension within your family.

CHAPTER 12

How to Gain Cheap Travel Budget in Retirement

Travel is among the best dreams for retirees. At this point, what feels enriching and fulfilling might be years of hard work to see new places or learn about cultures we have never experienced. Like I said in that other chapter, balancing this dream with money is super important to keep your travel plans fun and strong throughout retirement. We will explore the budget-conscious travel techniques you need to get on that plane and leave your financial woes behind. From planning advice to cost-saving hacks, you'll get valuable insights into making travel in retirement fun without costing a small fortune.

How To Create a Realistic Travel Budget

The first thing you need to do if you have dreams of traveling when you retire is create a travel budget. With a travel budget, you can make sure that the trips and experiences most important to you are funded BEFORE deciding on less significant vacations....

1. Set Your Travel Budget for the Year

First, estimate an attainable yearly travel budget you can handle with your finances. That spending plan should fit within your overall retirement financial blueprint — meaning that travel must not usurp other essential expenditures or long-term savings. Figure out how much you can afford to spend on travel each year from your discretionary funds.

Fixed vs. Flexible Spending: There might be specific trips or locations you are set on visiting no matter the cost and others that can vary based on how much fits your budget. For instance, you may take one big international trip on a fixed budget, while shorter, nearby, inexpensive trips can become more flexible.

All the Costs: Remember to budget for flights and hotels, food, getting around while there, entrance fees, souvenirs, and travel insurance. Itemizing these costs will help you avoid any nasty shocks later down the line when you are on the road.

2. Establish a "Travel Fund"

Having a travel fund makes budgeting simpler. Take a small fraction of your monthly earnings and earmark it for travel. Try to keep it in a separate savings account or perhaps even a high-yield one that generates interest on your travel money. This way, you know that money for a trip is always accounted for, and any planning can be done without feeling like it takes away from your other savings.

Tips for Affordable Travel

Cost-Effective Travel During Retirement It is very feasible to travel for cheap and not just stay somewhere but still have incredible experiences. Below, we will present some suggestions for easy travel without spending much money!

1. Off-Season Travel

The most basic money-saving travel tip is never to visit during high season. Flights, accommodation, and things to do can be much cheaper outside the high-density tourist season. For instance, flying to Europe in the fall or spring may be considerably more affordable than through mid-year. On top of that, there are fewer crowds, so sightseeing is more fun.

2. Explore Non-Traditional Types of Accommodation

Traditional hotels in hotspots can be pricey. The good news is that there are more affordable places to retire than ever.

Rentals: Airbnb and similar websites can provide apartments, single rooms, or entire homes, which also cost less than hotels. Vacation rentals come with a kitchen, which allows you to make your meals and save from eating out.

House Sitting By far, one of the most incredible ways for retirees to travel on a budget is by house-sitting. You can stay free for the roof over your head (and possibly with a pet-sitter job, their dogs, too). Platforms like Trusted House sitters connect homeowners to house sitters worldwide.

Home Exchange: If you are willing to trade homes by swapping yours with another traveler, services like Home Exchange can allow accessible accommodations at your site and their place consecutively into the future.

3. Look for Senior Discounts

Seniors can enjoy many senior discounts at airlines, hotels, and other travel companies. There are discounts on flights or cheaper entrances to museums, parks, and other attractions. When booking, always inquire if there is a senior discount. Sites like AARP can be a good source for retiree-centric deals with regular travel discounts.

4. Use the Public Transportation

City public transportation will almost always be cheaper than renting a car or paying for taxis. Many places will have longer-term discounted transit passes, and public transportation can make you feel more local. If you are considering traveling around for a bit, investigate rail passes or couch-surfing bus routes that pleasure at throwaway prices.

Extended Travel and Staycations

Retirement also allows you to travel for months to enjoy those experiences—and it's cheaper, too!

1. Long-Term Travel and Slow Tourism

Most of the time, you get better rates on accommodation if you plan to stay longer in a place. By the week or month, some vacation rentals also offer a weekly discount (10 to 15 percent), and significant savings can be had by staying put longer rather than jumping into town every couple of nights(null).

- Slow Travel Benefits:

Unlike merely passing through and spending a bunch of time on the road, you get to know one place, learn more about its culture, and experience what everyday life is like there. This method eases travel stress, saves transportation costs, and allows a slower pace.

- Regional Travel:

Regional travel is also inexpensive. It lets you make shorter trips close to your area, such as national parks, neighboring cities, or countryside retreats. These trips can be refreshing, and the price for a budget hotel will not even get you as far as flying out of town (or out of the country).

2. Embrace "Staycations"

A staycation can be every bit as fulfilling as an overseas trip. Explore Fun and Local Activities: Look for nearby places of interest you have not visited before, such as natural wonders or local festivals. By doing so, you can continue to save money while still experiencing something different and getting out of your regular routine.

Travel Planning Without Breaking the Bank

Travel is great, but only if you can sustain your travel planning and keep yourself financially healthy. Keep finances solid while embarking on the go.

1. Accept That You Have to Prioritize and Pace Yourself

You get motivated to travel and plan to go on so many trips. But making a budget and doing it at your own pace is key. Consider travel as an endurance sport, not a sprint. Instead of trying to plan one full trip as soon as possible, take the time and spread those dream trips out over a few years—it will give you a moment to breathe financially for once AND avoid travel burnout.

2. Travel Insurance | Must to Have for Mental Peace

Anything unforeseen, whether sickness or cancellations and loss of luggage, can happen during a planned trip, including those for retirees. Travel insurance protects your investment against emergencies, covering medical costs, trip cancellations, etc. Some policies will cover pre-existing medical conditions if the policy is taken out within a period after booking. It is an added expense, but travel insurance can be a huge relief and good protection, particularly for extended trips or overseas.

3. Preparation for Exchange rates and Currency Fees

If you go through an international airport, be facetious about exchange rates and lose money during currency conversations. If you do this, try to use a credit card without foreign transaction fees or negotiate ATMs with decent exchange rates. Checking exchange rates before your trip also lets you take the guesswork out of how much things will cost.

Keeping Your Financial Goals in Mind

Planning for the future While many are searching to explore, travel comes with a hefty price tag, and balancing that desire with long-term financial security means you may need to think carefully when booking those more extensive bucket list trips.

1. Do NOT use your savings or emergency funds

While it is sometimes tempting to go all out on the travel side of things, this latter option is significant because you first need to find a suitable working budget for flights and accommodation. Never Touch Your Emergency or Long-Term Savings for Travel Costs This also means that your travel adventures can't encroach on other financial goals or much-needed safety nets.

2. Working With A Budget: Be Flexible and Spontaneous

Planning is essential, but leaving room for spontaneity can make your trip more fun and affordable. They infuse an aspect of spontaneity into your travels, making them richer with things to do and having fun without breaking the bank. Leaving yourself a bit of wiggle room in your budget can help you create lasting memories without feeling the stress of breaking the bank.

CHAPTER 13

Adapting to Inflation in Retirement

Financial stability is even more important in retirement. However, predicting what the economy will do and how your investments will fare can be difficult. Fluctuations in the economy, inflation, and market volatility can impact savings and purchasing power, making it imperative to have a flexible approach toward financial management. One of the most challenging aspects of adapting to these changes for many people is finding a way when you are living on either a fixed income or reduced earning power due to retirement. Yet a resilient financial and life plan, when incorporating the right strategies, allows you to be secure at any moment in time so that there is peace of mind should changes occur. We will discuss practical ways to address inflation, guard against changing market conditions, and preserve optionality, applying these to your financial planning and lifestyle considerations. This will go a long way toward protecting your financial well-being and ensuring that you have the retirement you want to live.

What Inflation Means for Retirement

The White House and millions are now worrying about control of inflation. Even at mild levels, inflation can severely hurt the purchasing power of retirement funds compared to years before. This may not sound all that bad; however, after 20 years, the spending power of your savings will be halved in real terms if you do not include inflation in your financial planning.

1 Avoid unnecessary expencies

Well, one of the best strategies against inflation is preemptive strategy prep. In line with this tip, treat all your expenses as trees and build an annual COLA (cost of living adjustment) into the infrastructure budget, where you should aim to increase either income or spending power by a few percentage points each year.

Adjusting Withdrawal Rates: If you depend on a retirement portfolio for income, you might want to change your annual withdrawal rate to keep up with inflation. For example, if you initiate your retirement by drawing 4%, year-over inflation is almost 1-2%. But it is essential to remember how markets have been doing, as larger withdrawals during a down market can eat into your savings more quickly.

Inflation-Protected Assets: Buying TIPS with other inflation hedges, like tangible assets (real estate), can protect your purchasing power from eroding. While TIPS has built-in inflation, real estate goes up over time, so it's like an organic hedge against inflation.

2. Watching the Arbitrary Spending

Some expenses, such as healthcare, utilities, and groceries, often move faster than the overall average inflation rate. Many of these are essentials that comprise a big part of the budgets for many retirees. When planning, an "inflation buffer" specific to only such items can go a long way toward gaining financial security. Try to gradually add this annual inflation to your cost estimates; everyone makes an effort for not everything but at least a few places, so you do the same and try it here.

Fluctuations in the markets are par for the course, but as a retiree who may need to rely on your assets for their income (which is part of why we talk about how much you have managed to invest at retirement), these can be nerve-racking. The key is managing that exposure risk and having a strategy for these downturns so you can absorb them without drastically altering your lifestyle.

1. Risk Reduction through Diversified Investments

Diversification and Unsystematic Risk Management—It is well-known that a diversified portfolio protects the investor against market fluctuations. Holding a wide variety of asset classes—stocks, bonds (and cash, as well as maybe alternative investments like real estate or commodities)—reduces the effect of having any one segment in the market do poorly.

Since stocks should, on average, earn a higher return over time (and growth is valuable), the kind of balance we sought would allow for accumulation in both good and bad times. Nonetheless, as you enter the twilight of your investing years, some combination of bonds and cash equivalents in a portfolio can yield income with an acceptable amount of risk. Moving from functioning like the previous generation to becoming "financially sorted" for life is a balancing act. The trick is finding that sweet spot where your investment can weather fluctuations while providing you with long-term guarantees of addressing all the higher needs – especially as we live longer and on fast-track lives!

Regular Rebalancing: Market fluctuations can cause the proportions of your portfolio to deviate and unintentionally increase risk. By rebalancing—selling assets that have been borrowed and buying those that are lagging—you maintain your desired asset allocation, which keeps risk in check.

2. Save a Lot of Cash for Bear Markets

This is very useful during market slumps because you can refrain from selling every time the opposite happens when prices are meager and sometimes even loss-making. It provides a buffer for tough times, as this capital can fund your living expenses while your portfolio has the time to bounce back. The approach I see people use most often is maintaining 1-3 years of living expenses in a cash or low-risk liquid account, which could help mitigate the risk of selling investments during bear markets.

Reduce Sequence of Returns Risk: The sequence of returns risk is the threat that you could outlive your money because a severe bear market hits early in retirement and eats away at decades of portfolio appreciation. Keeping a cash reserve can help you shrink the percentage of your budget you withdraw in lousy stock market years so that more time is available for it to recover losses and reduce the chance that you might run out of money.

Flexible Financial and Life Planning: The Power of Adaptability

Understand Your Retirement Goals and Income Strategy, but remember you must be flexible and Able to adapt to support new changes without feeling like you are giving up the things that make life enjoyable.

1. I accepted this as simply different spending habits during early retirement.

Retirement expenses are not entirely predictable. Other years may come with more extraordinary healthcare expenses, while others are more about visiting or spending time with family. A flexible spending plan will allow you to adjust (s) without breaking a sweat.

Need/Want Spending: When you bucket expenditures into "essential" (necessary) and "discretionary," it becomes harder to spend on the latter. Things like housing, health care dollars, and utilities should be things we don't lightly touch, but they could shift up or down based on our financial situation.

Temporarily Modifying Withdrawal Rates: When markets are robust, you may wish to increase your withdrawals marginally or liberalize them just a bit. In periods of underperformance, reducing your withdrawal rate can allow you to extend the life of your savings and minimize selling pressure during these difficult times.

2. Building a Flexible Budget

This is one reason it pays to use a flexible budget rather than a fixed budget, like 50/30/20. Rather than having specific percentages or scales set for the categories, allow yourself flexibility in these areas. This way, you could increase the line for healthcare and your utility costs in higher inflation years but shrink down on those discretionary expenditures to balance out a sort of budget.

Exploring the "Core and Satellite" Approach– Budgeting on a Core and Satellite approach means splitting your budget between two parts: one is solid, fixed costs must-have items (core), and the second is for flexible cost adjustable overheads(satellite). This allows first to stabilize, second to save, and last preference for fine things in life.

Strategies for Financial Resilience Over a Lifetime

Although we cannot predict economic shifts, it remains entirely possible (and probably very wise) to survive such changes and thrive through a resilient financial system and strategic set of protocols for when the tides eventually evolve.

1. Creating Multiple Streams of Income

Having income sources outside of Social Security or making investment withdrawals provides a cushion that can help you weather financial storms. Think outside the box and give yourself flexibility by setting up multiple side incomes, such as a part-time job, rental income, or earning based on hobbies.

Income from Passions or Hobbies: If retirement frees you up to taking on part-time gigs, it might provide a chance to put money in your pocket through the things that pay based on passion, for example (or even if unavoidable). It rounds out you economically and keeps you rooted and activated. Perhaps you can capitalize on some of your hobbies, such as woodworking, crafting, consulting, or even tutoring, which would mean extra freelance income and give you the time to do what already excites you.

Passive Income: Dividend-paying stocks and real Estate Investment Trusts (REITs) pay regular payouts while conserving your assets.

2. Revising your financial plan periodically

Economic times shift, and so will your financial needs and goals. Even if there is no surge in the purchasing power of your portfolio, you must still revisit the retirement plan at least once a year to see how inflation has affected market conditions and other factors, then adjust it accordingly. This review helps you make some adjustments proactively, not reactively, by sustaining stability over some time.

Your Financial Advisor: A professional has the tools to give personalized insights about your goals and what is happening now. Advisors can guide intricate choices, like how to move money between accounts (asset allocation), tax-related issues, and new potential for income diversity.

Keep abreast of economic variables and financial products, as both can change over time. In addition, make sure you are informed of any changes in the law that could impact your retirement plan (new tax laws), Social Security modification, or investment opportunities. Catch you next time. In the interim, I hope this has made at least a few of those expenditures bubble up to your surface awareness so that you can begin making intentional decisions about where it is all headed.

CHAPTER 13

Adapting Technology in Retirement

New technologies have altered countless aspects of modern life — and, for retirees, this change is all for the better. Whether by helping people to keep in touch with loved ones (near or far) without leaving their homes or simply managing money and spending quick, easy pay transactions, recent technological innovations have provided features that will make retirement easier. But while digital is rapidly evolving? At the same time, it might prove to be overwhelming. So long as you can maintain a healthy balance and submit to only using devices or apps that improve your life, technology will be an invaluable tool in retirement. This chapter will reveal the practical uses of technology for ease and peace in everyday life, keeping in touch when you want to, and finding hobbies or interests.

Hopefully, technology, in moderation and with your eyes wide open toward the long-term side effects it can have on you as a senior, may help to add some joy (and sanity) into those so-called golden years.

Connection and Communication: Technology For The Socially Active

The beauty of technology is that it enables people to connect with loved ones, old friends, and even strangers anywhere in the world. Social interaction is essential for living a fulfilled life, and technology gives us easy ways to cultivate our connections.

1. Bridging the Gap Villeneuve said holding this second video call was all about connecting research communities during a hard time.

Video calling is now an essential communication tool, meaning you can interact just like face-to-face without being there. Free or low-cost video call options cover services like Zoom, FaceTime, and WhatsApp to remain socially distanced while connected with family members and friends whose laughs you sorely miss.

Maintain Regular Calls: Setting a date at least once every week or so, such as with loved ones, can offer excitement. Regular gatherings can include virtual holiday parties, family updates, or even themed calls where everyone contributes something special.

Joining Group Calls and Events: You may have the opportunity to participate in virtual gatherings like book clubs, exercise classes, and hobby groups within your community through video call platforms. This is a great way to meet new people, be involved, and find common interests with other like-minded peers.

2. Connection/Networking — Social media

On the one hand, social media sites (Facebook, Instagram, and LinkedIn, primarily) are great ways to keep in touch with kids, grandkids, or old friends you don't see all that much. They are small attempts to maintain, care for, and strengthen relationships: Post pictures, Comment on statuses, Update, Follow stories, and more.

Join Interest-Based Groups: Just like you have your communities in real life, people worldwide have groups they are a part of based on interests — gardening, travel, and local community events, to name just three. Joining these groups can help you make friends and socialize over mutual interests.

Privacy Settings: As much as you might want to reconnect with family and friends by going on a friend spree, everyone should feel comfortable using social media, so make sure your settings are set. To secure your privacy on these platforms, they provide facilities that allow you to control who sees what you post or become a friend and keep some of your private information out.

Technology for Daily Living and More

More than just helping you reach out to others, technology can streamline your daily life and make things more convenient. Digital tools that help with day-to-day tasks, shopping, and bill paying for health resources, digital can make every aspect of our lives easier.

1. Shopping online for convenience and access

Online shopping can be a good option for retirees to check prices, shop, and order from home without dealing with crowds. Online Shopping: From major online retailers like Amazon, Walmart, and Target to local grocery stores, as well as have consumer-friendly websites and apps.

You can set up subscription services—many retailers offer a choice for household items, groceries, or vitamins (so that you are automatically delivered on your chosen schedule). So, any of the aforelisted subscription services can be a great time-saver, and it will prevent you from running out of essentials.

Voice-activated devices for shopping lists: If you have an Amazon Alexa or Google Assistant device, you can create shopping lists without lifting one finger. This is great if you have mobility problems or need ease of use with verbal commands.

2. Online banking to keep your money safe

Online Banking—Online banking is the easiest and most convenient way to manage your Healthcare First Credit Union account. Follow this link for more info on Online Banking. View Account Balances, Transfer between accounts, or pay bills in just a few clicks! The convenient truth is that consumers use mobile banking, with most banks providing a secure platform and—OMG—automatic bill pay, direct deposit, and budgeting tools.

Configure Notification Dehydration: Some banking apps have notification alerts to inform you about significant transactions, low balances, or suspicious activity detected on your account. You can also enable alerts that provide another level of security without having to log in all the time or, more importantly, keep on top of your finances.

Budgeting Apps: Apps such as Mint or YNAB (You Need a Budget) allow you to track your spending and create a budget, which is very handy during the following step. With these apps, you can keep things organized and avoid using paperwork in your finances.

3. How to utilize telemedicine for health care services.

It is changing how you have access to a doctor, which is called telemedicine. While some in-person care may be necessary at your healthcare provider's office, many now offer virtual visits for routine check-ups and follow-up appointments — even quick health concerns. If traveling to appointments is inconvenient or challenging, using telemedicine services can help.

Health Metrics: I use Fitbit to track steps, heart rate, and other health metrics. These tools let you monitor your activity and goals and share data with healthcare professionals if necessary.

Keeping Track of Your Prescriptions: Medication reminders can be set up with apps like Medisafe to help you stay on track. You should create reminders to follow your medication schedule so you can take care of yourself as if you were in a hospital.

Developing New Hobbies and An Old Love of Learning

One of the best use cases for retirement is exploring new hobbies, learning something, or even re-invigorating old passions that took a back seat because you were busy with work. There are endless resources available to aid this vacation, from online courses in the technology domain to hobby-specific apps.

1. Skills Training & Personal Development Online Learning

Various e-learning platforms allow users to learn anything online, such as picking up a new language, enrolling in photography classes, or learning to play an instrument. Sites such as Coursera, Udemy, and Master Class are replete with lessons taught by leaders in virtually any field.

Interactive learning: You will also have the opportunity to attend Interactive classes, which allow you to interact with Instructors and peers. This helps you socialize while taking part in your class. Most platforms provide live sessions, discussion boards, and peer feedback-oriented courses.

USE FREE SERVICES: This may be a bit old school, but for the most part, I mean, stop reinventing the wheel. Many libraries and community centers offer online course access. Search for local colleges and universities with digital programs that allow students to take courses free of charge.

2. Further Hobby Enhancements with Targeted Apps

With interests in most hobbies, such as cooking, gardening, or painting, you can bet an app exists especially for them. Digital hobbies include apps like Yummy (for recipes), Garden Answers (to identify plants), or Procreate (for aspiring digital artists).

Take part in Digital Hobby Communities- Some graphic design apps have a community feature whereby users can interact using the app to share their work, ask questions, or learn from others. A connection that could drive your curiosity and the ability to relate with like-minded individuals.

Progress and Goal Tracking: Apps can also assist with progress tracking for hobbies that involve building skills. You can use a role-based system, each with features that allow you to set goals, see your progress, and celebrate milestones.

Staying Current Without Being Overwhelmed

Technology brings numerous advancements, yet the speed at which things evolve in the digital realm can feel like a lot to handle. The idea isn't to be great at every app and gadget but to use what is best for life.

1. Simple Devices, Easy to Use

opt for technology that seems effortless and intuitive. That said, you will always find a better experience with larger screens and easy-to-find settings, where tablets or smartphones work well. Accessibility features: Most significant brands provide some accessibility options, from larger text to voice control and screen contrast changes.

2. Establish Screen Time Limits

It can be tempting to become obsessed with tech as hundreds of social media platforms vie for our regard. Establish limitations on screen time and keep things balanced. You should set it aside at least one hour before bedtime, so program yourself for a "technology-free" experience.

3. Quality Over Quantity

It might be tempting to download a dozen apps or buy all the latest gadgets, but sticking with just a few tools you have found helps keep things under control. Use only apps or devices that make sense for your life, and do not buy into every new gadget because everyone else is.

4. Adopting a Learn as You go Attitude

With the changing technology landscape, there is no opportunity to learn everything now. Explore your new tools and ask friends, family members, or other online communities for advice. By slowly building up and favoring an intuitive approach to technology, the tension of needing to keep up will diminish.

CHAPTER 14

Living a Grateful and Content Life in Retirement

I see retirement is the time for deep contemplation and a more profound sense of fulfillment, where one achieves a complete cycle in life with grace & contentment. The ability to finally make peace with where you are and celebrate the small victories that give so much meaning, joy & depth. However, the joy of life may not be automatic — it is a mindset that can be developed by actively focusing on gratitude and what you have rather than dwelling on your past regrets or traumas. This chapter looks at ways to develop an attitude of gratitude and contentment in retirement. A life of gratitude and joy, from appreciating what you have to seeing the pleasure in experiencing little simple details, will make this stage more richly enjoyed and infinitely gratifying.

Contentment: Making Peace with Your Decisions

Happiness is not having everything go your way; happiness is accepting what comes and feeling peace within. Ponderings of inadequacy are counterintuitive and keep us from seeing the bigger picture. Worse still, when you approach retirement, perhaps it is then that we have more time to come full circle.

1. How Stereo mood Helped Me Cross this Bridge

Each one of us brings years and lifetimes of experiences, achievements, or even challenges accumulated over time. Viewing these experiences as significant and instrumental components of your walk can help you feel accomplished, satisfied, or proud. Review personal and professional growth moments that built resilience into your wisdom.

Write about your lived experience: by mining the gold from significant life events—what you have learned, how it has helped you to grow, and what similar material is there for which, of course, we inevitably be thankful—but that will help in helping us see all parts of our lives as they should be seen.

— Sara Delamont: It provides a sense of closure and acceptance, thus enabling you to look back with pride and satisfaction.

Share Your Story with Others—Celebrate your history with family or friends. You get a chance to look back and, through the media, pass on your lessons so that others can be like, "Oh, what makes sense?"

2. Letting Go of Regrets

It is okay to have regrets, but they can keep you from being fully present in the now. Being content is often about letting go of the remaining 'what ifs' and accepting that your choices come from a place of grace. Understand — whether you agree with the decision, that everyone was trying to do their best at a given time.

Forgiveness — of yourself so you can let go. Cut yourself slack, stepping back and appreciating that you gave it your best shot. Focus on the good that comes from your decisions rather than what you feel you missed out on.

Practice Mindfulness: Mindfulness is living in the moment, being present in what life actually means today rather than focusing on the past. Try meditating or doing other forms of mindfulness, like simple deep breathing, to find calm and acceptance through simply existing with your thoughts.

Celebration Small Wins: One key to a happy retirement is learning how to enjoy small victories and understand that making yourself happier isn't just about significant accomplishments that cascade/are founded one day. Small moments—morning coffee, a new novel, or a warm conversation—are the occurrences that make every day feel alive.

1. Unscrew Yourself > Recognize Daily Achievements

It can help restore feelings of purpose and accomplishment...Although the traditional milestones that used to define success, like career progression, may no longer be relevant in retirement, each day presents a chance to make satisfying connections with how we spend our time. Doing things around the house, learning something, or taking care of ourselves... all these small daily accomplishments that we do by ourselves increase motivation and reinforce a purpose.

Journal your "Wins" — Create a small victory journal where you write down your daily victories, even the tiniest ones. It can be as simple and wholesome as trying out a new recipe, completing that 500-piece puzzle you started last year, or looking after the plants in your garden. It will be a collection of lovely things you managed to do in the future.

Setting Simple Goals: Even though you are retired, consider creating little goals to get you out of bed in the mornings, like reading a book or finishing something around your house. It could be about health, hobbies, or maybe even social. Simple projects such as a daily walk, weekly call to a friend, or instrument learning are accomplished with practice and dedication to energy-related goals.

2. Appreciate the little things in life.

With retirement comes the gift of time, that magical resource that allows you to slow down and enjoy life. Enjoying/making fun of the now, without a frenetic schedule leading you around by your nose, makes everything more straightforward and pleasant.

Perform Mindful Activities: Perform activities that facilitate mindfulness, such as gardening, cooking, or even walking. Take some time to enjoy the sights, sounds, and sensations around you without distractions.

Celebrate Seasonal Changes and Nature: All seasons have their own beauty. Therefore, to be fulfilled, pay close attention to Nature during changes occurring with the Ninety Days Circle. Spending time at a nearby park, looking for birds, or watching the sunset are ways you can appreciate nature and separate yourself.

Developing a Gratitude Habit

Studies have indicated that a more profound sense of gratitude leads to greater overall well-being and life satisfaction -- you can work on building your gratitude muscle in retirement. Why practice gratitude? It reminds us of the joys in life and enforces peace or happiness.

1. Daily Gratitude Reflections

Regular daily reflection on what you are grateful for, however, forces a transition in the way you look at your life, helping lift even difficult days by reminding yourself of the good elements. Spend a few minutes daily thinking about things you are grateful for, including being well and having beautiful relationships.

Begin with Three Daily Gratitude:

Write a list of three things you appreciate daily. They can feel as simple as a good meal or a significant time with someone in your life. This is a quick practice that helps you solidify your grateful attitude.

Gratitude Thank You: Saying thank you to others by note, phone call, and in-person reminds you of the kindness all around. That appreciation validates and enriches the person you are showing love to but reinforces loving feelings within yourself.

2. Gratitude as a Weapon in your Time Of Need

Gratitude does not mean life is easy or perfect, but you have hope. In times of adversity, keep paying attention to what is still going right and let that be the ground on which you stand. For example, if health concerns or other reasons prevent us from doing the things we love, it may not be easy to lean on trust that all shall come as planned. So, when life puts obstacles in your path, and you cannot follow through with plans of action based on manifestation, look for gratitude instead.

Live Properly and Make the Most of Your Time

In the end, retirement happiness is as much about being present in this life with these people and enjoying what you have to look forward to in good health. You live in total and have a significant and happy life.

1. Build Real Relationships

Strong bonds knit a fulfilling retirement together. Llah spent with loved ones can provide shared moments and memories that add depth and joy to life.

Quality Time, Not Quantity: Spend quality time with them! You may feel free to engage in deep conversations over lunch, breakfast, or dinner. Laugh your bellies with each other—do not be silly, for God's sake, if humor does the work better and let it stay that way.

Everywhere... Be Open to New Friends: Retirement is a favorite time for Meeting new People. Expanding your social network can help you meet new people and gain many different perspectives, making life more colorful and stimulating.

2. Embrace Your Passions

Retirement should be a time to explore passions and interests or hobbies you have always wanted to try but never had the time for. Doing things that bring you happiness and a sense of fulfillment beautifies life daily, creating excitement each day.

Return to Old Hobbies or Begin Ones: If there is something you have always wanted, try your hobby again. It's probably not the same way about painting, playing an instrument, or going on tours, but engaging with things you cherish makes your life more content.

Pay It Forward: Many retirees are happiest when they pay it forward through volunteering time and resources, mentoring, or showing support for local causes. By helping others, we get purpose; they also feel happier and give us a sense of community, which makes the feelings of gratitude 5x times stronger.

CHAPTER 15

Best Investment Options to Consider When Approaching Retirement Age

Planning for life after work isn't just saving a set share of each paycheck; it involves deciding on placements that align with your later goals and offer the security and returns required with time. Selecting the proper assortment of investments can mean relaxing later or fretting before or after leaving the labor force. What's ideal relies on your risk threshold, earnings needs, and the way of life you envision in retirement. In this chapter, we'll explore investment possibilities before and after retiring. With an attentive strategy, you can maximize growth in your working years and shift to safer, income-focused selections as you enter retirement.

Grow your Wealth Before Retirement:
The years leading up to retirement invite taking advantage of longer investment horizons to build wealth by assuming more risk for potentially higher returns. Core to most retirement strategies stocks, historically offering the highest returns over the long term by investing in diversified stock funds and dividend-paying stocks for stability and passive income.

Real estate also presents opportunities for appreciation and rental income to establish a solid financial foundation. While stocks remain central, with diversified index funds spreading risk across industries, well-established dividend stocks provide regular payments and stability.

Meanwhile, rental properties demand active management but offer monthly proceeds, and property value increases if structuring responsibilities are acceptable. With a decade or more remaining, venturing into individual stocks or stock mutual and exchange-traded funds often yields significant growth. These premier investments harness compound growth and diversification during pre-retirement years focused on accumulating as much wealth as reasonably possible.

Real Estate Investment Trusts (REITs) offer hands-off property investing. By law, REITs that own and operate income-generating properties must distribute most profits as dividends. This makes them appealing for pre-retirement because shareholders gain returns without direct management duties.

Employer 401(k) accounts and Individual Retirement Accounts (IRAs) offer tax incentives that turbocharge savings growth. 401(k)s sometimes include matching funds, which are free money amplifying contributions. Getting the full match maximizes quick retirement accumulation. Traditional IRAs defer taxes on contributions until withdrawal, while Roth IRAs use post-tax dollars for tax-exempt distributions later on. Blending both IRA types furnishes versatility and tax breaks in the future.

As the departure date nears, securities with stability, like bonds, can balance a stock portfolio's risk. Bonds generate predictable yields appropriate for those transitioning to retirement life. Treasury bonds carry the full faith of the U.S. government behind them. Municipal bonds issued by cities or states offer tax benefits to certain bondholders. Both options fill the conservative portion of a pre-retirement investment mix seeking reduced volatility.

- Bond Funds:

These investment pools contain a variety of debt instruments, spreading risk across the bond market. They are ideal for those seeking exposure to fixed-income securities without picking individual bonds. While joining multiple bonds minimizes default risk, the value fluctuates as interest rates change. Some funds focus on specific maturities, like short-term bonds, avoiding sharp price drops if rates rise. Bond funds can introduce diversification when combined with stocks in a balanced portfolio.

After Retirement: Focusing on Income and Preservation

Once retired, growth shifts to protecting the principal and a steady income stream. Specific options stand out for those seeking this balance. Annuities provide guaranteed payments in a lifetime or for a set term. Immediate annuities start payments immediately in exchange for a lump sum, ensuring monthly income.

Fixed annuities lock in interest rates, preserving capital while earning modest returns without volatility. Dividend stocks remain favored for their regular income alongside potential appreciation. Established companies, especially utilities and consumer staples, typically offer dependable dividends, an attractive quality for retirees planning income. "Dividend Aristocrats," increasing dividends over 25+ consecutive years, instill confidence in a stable income stream, forming a retirement income core.

Bonds, particularly high-quality corporate or government bonds, also serve retirees through predictable income and relatively low risk. They supply stability, helping balance other assets and meet income needs in a manner less vulnerable to market fluctuations.

- Municipal Bonds

Issued by state and local governments, municipal bonds offer tax advantages for higher-income retirees seeking steady streams. While risks exist, experienced investors have long relied on munis to bolster pensions.

- Bond Ladders and CD Stratagems

Laddered bonds and CDs merit monitoring to preserve capital with predictable returns.

A bond ladder scatters maturities to smooth interest volatility; a CD ladder likewise provides periodic cash at a fixed increment. Savers thus split risks over time.

- Real Estate Strategies Evolve

Rental properties owned pre-retirement can sustain annuity-like flows. As workload weighs, outsourcing management warrants review. Selling and reinvesting proceeds diversify, too, whether in real estate investment trusts or relocating to lower-cost environs where savings go further. Managing assets migrates from active to passive as wanting less work proves wise.

Downsizing or Moving on Larger homes pose expenses that downsizing relieves; likewise, locations with cheaper living costs let nest eggs cover more. Tactical realignments like these free money to seed higher-yielding vehicles, delivering revenue streams supporting lifestyles with less labor over longer lifespans.

Balancing Growth and Security: A Hybrid Approach

Many retirees benefit from incorporating a hybrid strategy, maintaining a mix of income-producing holdings alongside growth investments. This diverse approach generates income while portioning your portfolio into assets with upside potential, helping shield against inflation.

1. Retaining a Stake in Equities

Keeping some of your portfolio in stocks makes sense even in retirement, particularly dividend-paying blue chips or stable growth plays. Equities provide a hedge against inflation and allow your assets to expand, ensuring funds don't run dry.

2. Managing Risk via Dynamic Rebalancing

It is prudent to periodically rebalance your allocation to align with your retirement objectives and risk profile. For example, if you retire with 60% in fixed income and 40% in equities, you might smoothly transition over time to a more conservative balance as your age advances.

CHAPTER 16

How to Spot & Avoid Wrong Investments

Investing is one of the best ways to become highly wealthy and cover yourself financially if something goes awry. Still, you must be very careful, for plenty of pitfalls are waiting to grab your money. Understanding the bad ones is just as critical as knowing what a good investment looks like. This will save you financially and keep your eye on the prize of what you set out to accomplish in the long term. This chapter will discuss actionable tips on identifying the warning signs and protecting your money-making ability by making better decisions.

Red Flags of a Bad Investment

The first step to protecting yourself before investing is understanding the signs of a bad deal. Here are some red flags indicating an investment might not be the best place to spend your money.

1. High returns guaranteed.

If an investment promises extraordinary returns with little or no risk, it is a dull red flag (lol). The truth is that investment returns are not guaranteed, and greater risk generally corresponds to higher returns. If you hear "guaranteed profits" or words like "risk-free returns," walk away.

- Assessing Risk and Return

A central tenet in investing is a payback between risk and return. Genuine investments in government bonds are safer and offer low returns. In contrast, higher returns are associated with more risk; consider it a payoff between returns and security, such as stocks or real estate.

- Beware of High-Pressure Sales Techniques:

Scammers often pressure victims to make an investment decision on the spot or rush them into making a financial commitment. Take a chill pill when rushed to get in or not miss out.

2. Detailed information about the investment

A real investment should provide complete information on the underlying asset, how it functions, and its related risks. When the fine print is as clear as air—or there is no fine print—it might be a red flag that you are jumping into something where things don't add up. All investments should come with clear documentation—it needs to be understood how this works, who manages it, and where your money is going. Avoid Investing If the investment is not clear.

Complex or "Off the Record" Strategies

Other investments could be unnecessarily complex, and you may not understand where your money is going. Be wary of an investment that has its basis in "proprietary" or "secret" strategies. Significant investments are transparent and easy to understand.

3. High Fees and Hidden Costs

Whether the fees killing your investment are high fees that eat away at its returns or hidden costs that turn what seems profitable on paper into a drag, chances are you invest money somewhere. Always make sure to look into the fee structure of any investing opportunity. If the fees appear too high or are not explicitly stated, walk away.

- Fees and How It Impacts Returns:

Every dollar you pay in fees is taken from your returns. For instance, certain mutual funds/managed accounts have management fees; others charge upfront or backend fees. Note: They also charge fees, so do some homework and determine how much these affect your total potential return.

- High Maintenance Fees:

Some investments clothe high fees in "maintenance" or "administration" charges. Ensure you know what each fee is for and whether it can be justified on the returns.

One particularly pernicious type of fraud involves illegal investment schemes, often appealing to those willing or looking for sky-high returns with little associated risk. We must identify these scams to avoid taking our money from us.

1. Ponzi and Pyramid Schemes

Ponzi and pyramid schemes attract investors with the promise of high returns. They often use the money of newly recruited investors to pay earlier investors' promised profits. These pyramid deals fall apart when they run out of new people to scam.

How to Know When You Have Been In A Ponzi Scheme:

If you see natural cause, this should be just an indicator since if the businessman is excellent, he can know how to minimize his losses by doing other sorts of business and receive (let us say) 10% return per month quite consistently. If you're promised consistent, above-market return in one investment, but its strategy is the market itself or a more straightforward part of it, be very skeptical.

Signs of a pyramid scheme: In the short term, it looks like a chicken and egg problem because recruitment is more important than the investment itself. The person who tries to get you in then will say, no....you actually make money by inviting more people into the program and not off of an underlying asset (i.e., your sales results)……..(that is a pyramid scheme)

2. Pump-and-Dump Scams

Pump-and-Dumps: A park-and-d therapist is a stock that trades at high prices, paying investors very hot shares (the case also stars tally mojo as sil average of its investor via investing in other statuzuko or partures with a lot in rises are pumped before statement stolen price is able out).

Pump-and-dump scams are a regular occurrence in penny stocks or unlisted companies, so don't spend your hard-earned money on something someone calls "hot." Hot stock tips or unsolicited advice from people (unfamiliar) is a caution sign to beware! Do your analysis on all investment recommendations.

Properly Researching Stocks Before Buying: You should always research a stock's fundamentals, whether earnings, market fit, or industry trends. A sharp-up move in a stock price for no apparent reason is dangerous territory.

3. Unlicensed vendors and unregistered investments

Always check if the person or company you want to invest through is licensed and registered with reputable regulatory bodies. For example, here in the UU, it is registered with the Securities and Exchange Commission (SEC) or a state securities regulator.

Are They a Pro: Determine if the financial professional is registered with sites like

FINRA's Broker Check in the U.S. This tool runs a background check on brokers and advisors, including any disciplinary actions.

Steer Clear Of "Off-the-Books" Proposed Investments: If someone tries to entice you into investing your money with them directly rather than a bonafide financial institution, TREAD CAUTIOUSLY. Tangible investments are permanently recorded and tracked through natural systems.

Best Ways to Safeguard Your Investments

Preventing the worst investments isn't just about recognizing red flags; it also requires proactive measures to safeguard yourself and your financial future.

1. Conduct Thorough Research

Never invest without research. Investigate the investment, who is behind it, and how it interacts with your goals. And that is your best protection against making untimely investment decisions.

Seek Out Independent Sources Of Information:

Base your investment decisions on information from independent sources, not just the person or company that wants you to invest. Find third-party news articles, reports by analysts, and industry reviews to see if others are saying anything about the legitimacy or success of an investment.

Question Everything: Never hesitate to ask detailed questions about an investment's structure, risk, and potential reward. If the answers are general or unsatisfactory, this is a signal to be red-flagged.

2. Stick to What You Understand

Invest in what you know — one of the best defenses against lousy investments. Many of the best investments you can make are often very simple and extremely easy to understand what they do. If something is too complicated to understand, it can hide risk.

Should Invest in Familiar Assets: Many investors prefer investing in types of assets they know, such as stocks and bonds. Investing in what you see drastically decreases your chances of becoming involved with something that (a) will work out poorly for investors over the long term because those things have been well picked over. So, sectors where people are clueless about many companies involve situations they can't possibly evaluate correctly.

Stick to Low-Quality Investments Unless You Know: High-risk investments like options trading, cryptocurrencies, or leveraged funds can be complex and require a different skill set. If you are a beginning investor or prefer to play it passively, this is best avoided until another day.

3. Always get in touch with a reliable financial advisor

An independent financial advisor can also become a useful one, especially when it comes to investments. As part of a larger team, you can get advice from dedicated professional advisors who understand your financial goals and appetite for risk, sparing you the potential pitfalls of bad investments.

Subscribe to a Premium Financial Advisor:

If you need help getting started and maybe even some advice from time to time but not management, going with the Minimum service might be all you require. That is an essential protection because fiduciary investment professionals are less likely to sell you investments they get a commission on or personally benefit from.

Get a Second Opinion:

Always ask another professional to confirm what was said or propose something new. An outside perspective could be just the thing you need to clear your head and know that going through with it would lead in a dangerous direction.

www.ingramcontent.com/pod-product-compliance
Lightning Source LLC
Chambersburg PA
CBHW052351220526
45465CB00003BA/1057